Race
and
Theology

PRAISE FOR ELAINE A. ROBINSON'S RACE AND THEOLOGY

With *Race and Theology*, Elaine A. Robinson provides a critical resource for understanding the ways that race and racism have distorted the Christian faith in North America. More important, the book offers insights for what we might do about this distortion. By offering an analysis of the frequently used but often wrongly conflated ideas of race and racism, Robinson uncovers the ways that oppressive social powers often flourish in contexts where well-meaning people would wish otherwise. In her unfolding of this analysis, Robinson introduces us not only to some of the more important theologians and theorists of our day but also to what it means to expand this conversation beyond simply black and white. In all, an important work that is useful to both academic and more popular conversations about the content of faithfulness in a race-conscious society.

—Stephen G. Ray Jr., Professor of Systematic Theology, Neal A. and Ila F. Fisher Chair of Theology, Garrett-Evangelical Theological Seminary; and Executive Director, the Society for the Study of Black Religion

An extraordinary resource for understanding how mainline U.S. constructed Christianity has privileged whiteness at the expense of all others. This volume is vital for those who want to join the liberationist ranks as allies so we can free our faith from racism and further the work of social transformation in the changing U.S. context.

—Stacey M. Floyd-Thomas, Associate Professor of Ethics and Society, Vanderbilt University, Executive Director of the Society of Christian Ethics and the Black Religious Scholars Group

HORIZONS IN THEOLOGY

Race and Theology

ELAINE A. ROBINSON

Abingdon Press
Nashville

RACE AND THEOLOGY
Copyright © 2012 by Abingdon Press

This book is printed on acid-free paper.

Library of Congress Cataloging-in-Publication Data has been requested.

ISBN 978-0-687-49425-5

12 13 14 15 16 17 18 19 20 21—10 9 8 7 6 5 4 3 2 1

MANUFACTURED IN THE UNITED STATES OF AMERICA

CONTENTS

ACKNOWLEDGMENTS

I t takes a village to raise a child, but several villages to raise a white theologian whose concern is to dismantle racism through a process of sustained engagement in racialized discourse and practice. Numerous persons and communities have shared in the writing of this book, some directly and others by helping to deepen my understanding of fully human existence in the context of the United States.

Several colleagues at Saint Paul School of Theology have provided encouragement for this project. In particular, I wish to thank Dr. Myron McCoy, Drs. Patti and Shannon Jung, and especially Dr. Angela Sims, who has been a valued conversation partner on the subject of race and racism. My colleagues and friends Drs. Stacey and Juan Floyd-Thomas of Vanderbilt University have been instrumental in this journey in more ways than I can express in words. It is my prayer that Lillian Makeda may grow up in a radically transformed world.

My colleagues in the Oklahoma Conference of The United Methodist Church energize and sustain my ministry at Saint Paul in countless ways. Bishop Robert E. Hayes Jr. embodies faithful servant leadership, and I am blessed by his example and friendship. The men and women of the extended cabinet, the pastoral leaders, and the laity encourage me to fulfill my calling, often overlooking my many shortcomings. I am grateful for sharing in ministry with you.

The communities of color that have surrounded me with their faith and prayers and helped my nascent double consciousness take shape include members of the Oklahoma Indian Missionary Conference, Nueva Vida United Methodist Church in Fort Worth, Texas, and

1

Quayle United Methodist Church in Oklahoma City under the leadership of Dr. Victor McCullough. The Reverend David Wilson, the Reverend Anita Phillips, and the Reverend Chebon Kernell have been sources of inspiration and deep reflection on the relationship of Christianity to Native Americans. Their wisdom and support have been essential to the creation of a Native American Ministries program at Saint Paul School of Theology at OCU. *Gracias a mis hermanos y hermanas en Nueva Vida, Francisco Salinas, Ricardo Torres, y especialmente Cordélia y Ernesto Gutiérrez. También, Rev. Sandra Cabrera ha sido una hermana en la fe hace muchos años.* We shared a truly miraculous journey together, believing in the power of God to renew and sustain the church. And to the most faithful members of the Friday morning study group at Quayle—Sisters and Brothers Jessie Davis Wesley, Jacqueline Devereaux, Sharon Harris-Klein, Leonard Benton, Jan Crump, and Glenn Harris—thank you for what you've taught me and for the laughter and insightful conversations we've shared.

Finally, thanks to my editor at Abingdon Press, Kathy Armistead, for suggesting that I write this book, and to my team in Oklahoma City who gave me the space to complete the manuscript and kept the campus running smoothly: the Reverend Rick Burns, Rachel McClain, and the Reverend Tari Carbaugh.

I am blessed to be surrounded by a circle of life-giving communities.

FOREWORD

In the end, we will remember not the words of our enemies,
but the silence of our friends.

—Martin Luther King Jr.

In light of King's words in the epigraph, we write this foreword as we observe, celebrate, and lament his legacy in the midst of a time when the work of race relations, liberation theology, and the church's relevance have many people questioning if his dream was, in fact, deferred. But, after reading Robinson's *Race and Theology*, we are indeed reminded that even in the sounds of silence, the voice of one ally can indeed hew "a stone of hope" "out of the mountain of despair." Elaine Robinson's contribution embodies this hope.

If we listen to opinion in the public square, we're in a post-racial era, and political pundits and private profiteers alike claim that racism is something of the past and is nothing more than a *belief* of racial superiority manifested as prejudice and/or discrimination. If true, we can then argue that racism no longer exists. After all, who among us really believes that their race is superior to other races?

While at one time, specifically during the heyday of Jim and Jane Crow systemic racial segregation, most white Americans accepted their race to be superior to others. Although decades of political correctness have led most whites today to reject such racialized beliefs, yet there are still neo-Nazis skinheads, Ku Klux Klan members, and reactionary right-wing media pundits. Overall, however, most whites, especially the young, seem to earnestly reject the belief of racial superiority. As proof of this rejection as well as the fact that we, indeed, live in a new post-everything era, many observers point to voting for the first black man (albeit son of a white woman) to become president of the United States. By this token, doesn't Obama prove racism no longer exists?

And yet to argue that racism and ethnic discrimination is a thing of the past is problematic, offending our sense of discerning the obvious. Without a shadow of a doubt, every social scientific study ever conducted reveals that racism and ethnic discrimination is alive and well within the United States. When compared to their white counterparts, people of color continue to be poorer, hungrier, and more destitute according to all social and economic indicators. No doubt some persons of color may have grasped the brass ring, but for the disproportionate majority, life continues to be lived in disenfranchisement and marginalization. The very fact that we do not refer to President Obama, the son of a black man, as a white man clearly illustrates how the one-drop rule—the cultural premise that a drop of "black" blood is enough to "pollute" the whole—has normalized and legitimized how we see and define reality.

But how can racism continue to be a common experience among people of color if most whites reject the belief of white supremacy? As long as we define racism as a belief manifested as bigotry, then no progress will ever be made in dismantling it. Or, put it another way, racism can never be reduced to simply a belief; rather it is a social structure in its own regard. In fact, whites could be nonracist allies who may have even marched with Martin Luther King Jr., or stood alongside Cesar Chavez, and yet they continue to benefit within this society because of their white skin pigmentation and the societal privileges bequeathed to them because of their whiteness. Belief has little to do with racism since, regardless of a white person's beliefs, the social structures constructed since the foundation of the United States have been fully articulated toward racist ends. And even when they attempt to dismantle these very structures designed to privilege them, would-be white allies run the risk of having those same structures turn against them in devastating manners in order to protect the primacy of whiteness.

Social structures that protect the white supremacist ideal, privileging those who are closest to whiteness (even within racial and ethnic communities) are woven into the very tapestry of life within these United States. Every aspect of US life, including religious life, is undergirded

4

with principles that promote, protect, and privilege whiteness. Yet, not surprisingly, a decade into the new millennium we still find that the Sunday church hour remains the most segregated hour of the week. Not only is the church segregated, but so are our seminaries, theological centers, and religious discourses. For many, the hope of diversification is more for the sake of political correctness than intellectual prowess, for after all, if publishing and academic hiring from communities of color is done for the sake of scholastic excellence, it would then mean that most publishing houses and schools that lack this presence also lack intellectual rigor.

Those who have been born within an Euro-American culture are products of a society wherein white supremacy has historically been intertwined with how Americans have been conditioned to see and organize the religious world around them. Scholarship within the field of religion remains a constructed discourse, legitimized and normalized by those who have the ways and means to make their subjectivity objective, hence, determining who is "in" (academically rigorous) and who is "out" (interesting perspective but lacking academic excellence). The scholarship emanating from communities of color that specifically challenge the racialization of our discipline are usually relegated to interesting perspectives or simply ignored. Whether consciously or not, the racist assumptions of the dominant culture influence how they develop and participate in the prevailing academic discourse on religion.

One can be awarded a PhD in religion without ever having to know, understand, or even read any of the scholarship produced by scholars of color; nevertheless, one can never pass comprehensive exams without mastering the dominant Eurocentric canon. The quest for "academic excellence" operates as code-language for fluency in Eurocentric meta-narratives. It is bad enough that scholars of color are physically invisible from scholarly production as made evident whenever one peruses most academic syllabi. This situation is further exacerbated by their absence from most religion departments and schools of theology. Is it any wonder that so few white scholars engage communities of color even when discussing or writing about the dismantling of racism? Fortunately, the book you are holding in your hands is not one of those that name a few scholars of color for the sake of decorum and appearances without actually ever engaging their work.

To this point, Elaine Robinson is one of those few antiracist allies who seriously consider the work that arises from the margins of society. Rather than simply reducing racism to some bigoted belief, she attempts to raise the consciousness of her white colleagues about how racism is a perennial structural problem that impacts both the society and how religion is done by Christians, while remaining in conversation with those communities most devastated by racism and ethnic discrimination. *Race and Theology* is an important contribution to the discourse because it unmasks and debunks a US-constructed Christianity that for too many years has privileged whiteness at the expense of all others. This volume is a compelling read that moves the conversation forward!

Miguel A. De La Torre
Stacey M. Floyd-Thomas
*On the evening of the Day of Observance of
the Reverend Dr. Martin Luther King Jr. 2012*

INTRODUCTION

White theologians and philosophers write numerous articles and books on theodicy, asking why God permits massive suffering, but they hardly ever mention the horrendous crimes Whites have committed against people of color in the modern world. Why do White theologians ignore racism?

—James H. Cone

In his *Prescription against Heretics*, Tertullian penned his memorable and influential question, "What indeed has Athens to do with Jerusalem?" In the late second century, Tertullian posited an antithetical relationship between the Greek philosophical tradition and scriptural Christianity. Of course, later interpreters of Tertullian's writings recognize his dependence upon philosophical speculation such that his privileging of Christian doctrine may not represent the anti-intellectualism some have supposed. Nonetheless, the positioning of Athens versus Jerusalem has raised questions, at various points in Christian history, about the relationship of philosophy to theology and Scripture, even if most contemporary theologians do not consider philosophical or scientific knowledge to be in opposition to Christian faith.

Today, in the twenty-first century, the question to be raised in Tertullian-like fashion is simply: What have race and racism to do with theology? Some, perhaps most, will argue that in a perfect world the appropriate answer would be nothing, but the reality of corrupt reason and human nature suggests we cannot turn a blind eye to the relationship between the two, especially if our desire is to eliminate racist discourse and practice from theology and ecclesial organizations. Since the 1970s and the appearance of James Cone's, *Black Theology and Black Power,* the first book on liberation theology ever published, theologians of color in the United States have argued for the persistence of racialized and racist logic and discourse in theological writings, particularly those of white theologians.* Cone has characterized racism as America's "original sin."[1] Yet, white theologians have largely remained silent on the question of racism, thereby suggesting, perhaps, that racism is not an appropriate consideration for Christian theology or, at least, not one they wish to engage.

I first encountered liberation theology and the question of racism and white privilege as a first-year seminary student in an introduction to theological studies taught by Schubert Ogden. One of the assigned readings toward the end of the semester—and the only assigned reading I remember to this day—was James Cone's essay "God is Black," excerpted from *A Black Theology of Liberation* and published in *Lift Every Voice.*[2] Many of my peers had emotionally-charged reactions to Cone's argument (as have many of my own students in introductory courses, despite my advance warnings to contextualize the essay and simply try to remain objective), but I found the theology provocative and exciting. To be sure, as a neophyte at theological inquiry, I did not fully grasp the content of "God is Black." But it began a personal journey of understanding, of conscientization, and of seeking to break open the logic of white privilege. I have attempted to become black by the grace of God, despite my white skin. But I have encountered discomfort and "disease" with my decision to locate myself intellectually, spiritually, and physically on the margins, among communities and scholars of color and their writings. In the United States, most people would rather discuss anything but race and racism. It is an observation that can generally be applied to theologians, pastors, and the Christian faithful who remain reluctant to examine racist and racialized discourse and practice in the church and beyond.

---

* In the pages to follow, "white" will refer to persons of European and Anglo descent unless otherwise noted. Whiteness is complicated by the fact that persons who are not descended from Europe or the British Isles can pass for "white" in the United States and enjoy the unearned privileges accruing to it.

Cone has repeatedly expressed dismay at this ongoing phenomenon. Why won't white theologians take racism seriously? In his 2004 essay, "Theology's Great Sin," Cone posits four main reasons for the silence of the theologians. First, "Whites do not talk about racism because they do not have to talk about it."[3] This fact arises out of the power that whites, as the majority culture in society, hold in relation to other minoritized racial and ethnic persons.[4] This power extends across the political, social, cultural, intellectual, and religious spectrum. Too few theologians are willing to acknowledge their complicity with systemic powers that create and sustain racial disparities.

The second source of silence, according to Cone, is guilt. Guilt is an emotion rooted in the intellectual awareness of how white privilege operates at the expense of persons of color. Wealth and economic prosperity, opportunities for advancement, and other advantages accruing to whiteness were built upon black labor and red land. But most white people repeat the oft-heard protest or disclaimer that neither they nor their direct ancestors were slaveholders or stole the land of Native peoples. Most whites understand themselves as "color-blind" and able to treat all persons equally. Thus, there exists a denial of white privilege because it weighs heavily upon those who acknowledge its existence. To name white privilege is to admit to possessing unearned advantages.

Cone then offers a third source of silence with regard to America's long history of racism: the fear of black rage. Acknowledging that the "spirit of Black theology was closer to [the language of] Malcolm than Martin," Cone recognizes the discomfort whites experience when African Americans speak with passion. In fact, he argues that whites "cared more about White emotional comfort than the suffering of the Black poor."[5] White society does not engage in conversation around the issue of reparations for the centuries of enslavement, Jim Crow laws, lynchings, and poverty. Cone concludes that, "Our future depends on [whites and blacks working together]. But that can never happen creatively until Whites truly believe that their humanity is at stake in the struggle for racial justice."[6] This notion that white people are less than fully human when participating in systemic racism is a key concept to which we will return in subsequent chapters.

Finally, white theologians remain silent about racial justice "because they are not prepared for a radical redistribution of wealth and power."[7] White privilege is prevalent and provides for distinct advantages, which white theologians and white Christians do not wish to relinquish. Even progressive Christians are complicit: "Progressive Whites do not mind talking as long as it does not cost much, as long as the structures of power remain intact."[8] But if systemic privilege and marginalization remain unchanged, the racist discourse and practice of America will continue unabated. The implicit question raised by Cone's analysis is whether white Christians prefer their privilege and status to the justice and full humanity demanded by the gospel of Jesus Christ.

To address the question of racism in relation to theology is to enter a complex conversation in which religion, race, context, politics, economics, and power intertwine. Even as Cone highlights key issues, responses to his analysis—and at times his own writings—do not delve deeply enough into the thicket of theology's collusion with political, economic, and cultural norms over the past four hundred years. Clearly, centuries of collusion cannot be dismantled overnight, but this reality has yet to be widely exposed, acknowledged, and analyzed, which constitutes the first step in dismantling systemic racism in the United States. Lacking conscientization, white theology has yet to take seriously its need to engage in racialized discourse, defined as that which uncovers, analyzes, and dismantles racism. Consequently, this neglect serves to undermine the truthfulness and credibility of the theological task in the contemporary era.

Despite the long-standing collusion, which might be identified as sins of commission and omission, race is seldom discussed in polite company or in institutions shaped by the white majority culture. If religion, politics, and sex are excluded topics at the dinner table or polite company, race and racism do not even make the list of banished topics. Good church people always claim to love everyone. But if Sunday morning continues to be the most segregated time of the week in the United States, if mainline Protestant denominations continue to have racial and ethnic caucuses in order for the perspectives of Christians of color to be vocalized, if churches are taking stands on immigration, education, or unemployment, then race is likely to be part of the analysis, even if it remains unnamed. If theologians do not address the question of race, the implicit message to church members and leaders is that race and racism are not theological or ecclesial matters. If this is the case, then how will it be possible for churches to enter into thoughtful reflection upon the rapidly changing demographics of the United States and the church's failure to serve and represent the general population? Even as the mainline denominations dwindle and the need to reach a growing nonwhite demographic is apparent, theology provides few resources to facilitate the church's reflection. Theology, long considered as reflection upon the first order discourse of the church, has the distinctive task of reflection that serves as a critical corrective to ecclesial practice, whether prophetic or priestly in nature. So why do white theologians turn a blind eye to racist practices, discourse, and logic of the church?

If Cone's analysis is even partially correct, then theology's task is clear: it must address the question of racism. Theology has the task of acknowledging its collusion with society's and the church's long history of racism, as well as identifying and describing the ways racialized discourse and practice can become manifest in the contemporary setting as a corrective. Only then can theologians and churches undertake the urgent task of constructing theological discourse that dismantles white privilege and white supremacy and contributes to ecclesial practices that further the reign of God on earth and the full humanity of all persons.

What, then, have race and racism to do with theology? In the following chapters, we will begin to expose the complexity of this question and the ways in which theology and racism have been and remain entangled. For too long theology, particularly *white* theology—or what I will rename as "theologies of privilege" in the last chapter—has largely sidestepped racial considerations as irrelevant or, at best, marginal to the theological task. This short exploration suggests that, to the contrary, exposing and dismantling racism may represent the most pressing theological task of the twenty-first century. I will argue that as long as racist discourse and practice continue to shape the church and society in the United States, theologians have an urgent calling to engage in racialized discourse and practice, defined as that which uncovers, analyzes, and dismantles racism.[9] These distinctions will be central throughout the following chapters.

In chapter 1, preliminaries related to racism and theology are introduced. The contours of racism, white privilege, and white supremacy are examined as a necessary basis for the argument to proceed into theological considerations. Particularly important is the notion that the very nature of Christianity and, therefore, theology as represented in the early Jesus movement, shifted as it became a function of the state and the privileged members of society under Constantine the Great.

Chapter 2 examines theological anthropology, as constructed by theologians of color and white theologians, under the assumption that Christianity in collusion with racist discourse and practice has contributed to the dehumanization of countless persons within the United States. While theologians of color expose racist discourse and

11

practice through continual engagement in racialized discourse and practice as central to the meaning of fully human existence in this country, white theologians remain largely reticent, under the guise of neutrality, when it comes to naming and dismantling racism in their own theologies and the church. Central to this chapter is the assumption that both white Americans and persons of color are dehumanized and cannot be fully human as created by God unless the systemic sin of racism is exposed and its elimination is pursued as a basic Christian vocation.

In chapter 3, the history of racism in relationship to economics, politics, and theology is traced utilizing Cornel West's methodology of demythologizing and demystifying. Three distinct periods of racist and racialized history emerge. In the era prior to the Civil War and the Fourteenth Amendment to the Constitution, the prevailing question was simply whether nonwhite peoples were human. This overt attempt to dehumanize dominated the racist constructions of human beings and found widespread theological justification. In this first period, theology was, in large measure (though never entirely), guilty of sins of commission. The period from 1865 until civil rights legislation was enacted represents the second phase of racist and racialized discourse and practice, in which theology largely became silent and allowed the "scientific" study of race to offer evidence of the white race's superiority, even if evidence concluded that persons of color and white people belong to the same species. Theology's sin—or that of theologies of privilege—became one of omission, even as some theologians provided counter narratives decrying this dehumanization. Finally, after 1965, the era of "modern racism" began. While voices of color emerge on the scene in ever greater numbers, white theologians often mirror society's false assumption that the playing field has been leveled by legislative fiat, thereby resulting in a stance of "neutrality" around issues of race. White theologians tend to perpetuate the sin of omission, using the cover of legal rights to shroud the question of racism in the church and society, as well as their own theologies. Yet, theologians of color continue to expose the façade of this logic.

In the concluding chapter, we turn constructively to the question: Will theology and white theology in particular enter into racialized discourse and practice in order to shape the emerging historical era in light of the full humanity of all persons? In response, we will propose three modes of restoration and three theological tasks which include conscientization, an ethical corrective or component within theological discourse, and theological reparations. White theology faces a critical moment. It can choose to remain stubbornly mute with regard to its history of racism or it can choose to reconstruct its discourse in order to participate in the flourishing of all persons and a new social and systemic reality that more closely mirrors the reign of God on earth.

1

AMERICA'S ORIGINAL SIN

Racism is particularly alive and well in America. It is America's original sin and it is institutionalized at all levels of society.
—*James H. Cone*

One must suppose that in order to feel comfortable in the Christian faith, whites needed theologians to interpret the gospel in a way that would not require them to acknowledge white supremacy as America's great sin.
—*James H. Cone*

Since the colonists first set foot on the shores of the New World down to the present day, racism has been a major motif in the narrative of the United States. It is, as theologian James Cone has suggested, America's "original sin." For a country founded on freedom, democracy, and equality, the racist history appears paradoxical.[1] For a country that has been predominantly Protestant over the centuries, the racist history seemingly belies the notion that the United States is a "Christian" nation, for the love of God and neighbor can never serve as motivation for racist practices and rhetoric. Yet, democracy, Christianity, and racism have been intertwined for centuries. Any exploration of race, racism, and race relations in the United States demands a level of analysis that integrates the interlocking factors of politics, economics, religion, and power. There would be no racist history if not for the political and economic exigencies and objectives entangled with Christian theologies and biblical interpretations. Hence, untangling this knot has the potential to reform theological discourse in ways that more closely reflect the pre-Constantinian Jesus movement in the context of the contemporary setting.

What Is Racism?

Racism is at heart about differentiation and evaluation of superiority and inferiority based largely upon physical characteristics such as skin color, eye shape, hair texture, and visible cultural characteristics such as language and clothing. Often, racism is conceived of as an individual belief or practice reflecting a personal moral failure. Under this logic, a person who dislikes or discriminates against others based upon their race is considered a racist. Thus, one can position one's self as neutral or set apart from racist practices, history, and discourse by forwarding the claim, "I love everyone equally" or "I never _____ (owned any slaves), (took land from any American Indians), (interned any Japanese-Americans in World War II)," or more mundanely "(prevented any person of a different race from attending my church)." While individual racism is never to be condoned, when racism is construed as only an individual moral failure, a personal sin, then alibis abound and few racists exist today.[2]

Racism, however, is a socially structured, systemic reality and must be approached on this level of analysis. Within the United States, racialized practices and logic are embedded in corporate entities, educational institutions, governmental policies, ecclesial bodies, and the mass media. Claiming ignorance or individual innocence serves only to reinforce the systemic nature of racism. Systemic or structural sin thereby suggests that society requires a form of repentance and redemption. It suggests that no earthly principality or power, nation or state, confederation or republic can ever represent the reign of God on earth. Some, indeed, may better express a life-furthering rather than death-dealing nature, but even the best human institutions will be subject to corruption and the seductions of worldly power. The Hebrew Scriptures are rife with examples of God's "chosen people" pursuing worldly ways only to be called to repentance and restoration. The church is no exception, which is why theologians such as Schleiermacher and Tillich considered the Reformation a continual process of repentance and re-formation.

Thus, racism is not simply prejudice against different races, but is a product of power differentials within society. It suggests that racist discourse and practice enables some to prosper at the expense of others. Racism reflects the ability of one race to dominate other races based upon the logic of superiority and inferiority, and this power is vested in systems and structures that perpetuate, maintain, and re-create the divisions. The term "racism" was first used in the late 1920s in reference to the rise of the Nazis in Germany. By 1945, this regime would manifest itself clearly as a systemic form of prejudice, differentiation, power, and unimaginable evil, and it remains one of the most obvious, overt examples of systemic racist discourse and practice.[3] There, too, politics, economics, race, religion, and power were interwoven. To reiterate, racism simply cannot be examined adequately in isolation from this complex web of relations.

Despite evidence to support the notion of systemic or institutional racism, this level of analysis remains under interrogation by scholars and generally unrecognized by the larger public of the United States. Although his argument focuses primarily, though not exclusively, on British society, Ali Rattansi argues that analyses of institutional racism inevitably fail to investigate the relationship of racialized practices to issues of class and gender and other complex phenomena. In Rattansi's view, "strong racism" or "hard racism" is defined "as the belief that separate, distinct, biologically defined races exist; that they can be hierarchically ordered on the basis of innate, and thus unalterable superior and inferior characteristics and abilities; and that hostility is natural between these races."[4] Strong racism is no longer a tenable position, as the quest to discover a scientific basis for such beliefs has failed. Even though race is not a scientifically verifiable reality, racism continues to be a much discussed and often alleged feature of advanced societies. How then can one speak of racial discrimination in a "post-race" world? Rattansi argues that institutional racism is more likely to be a combination of factors that result in discrimination, and the term "racism" is misleading and should be abandoned.

In lieu of the maligned concept of racism, Rattansi proposes the use of the social scientific term "racialization" as a more apt concept. Racialization focuses on the degree or extent of racism or "racisms," particularly factors of strong racism, present in any situation or case of systemic racism. It moves away from the simplistic binary pattern of racist or not racist to discern degrees of racialized practice or discourse.[5] Attention to racialization thus allows us to take into account arguments based on some form of biological determinism and cultural patterns, as well as to blur the superior/inferior distinctions since some racial stereotypes—the "clever Jew," for instance—do not lend themselves to neat categorizations.[6] Although Rattansi does not pursue the notion of theological discourse, it could also be investigated as a dynamic within this concept of racialization and, in keeping with the argument at hand, should be investigated.

Rattansi's argument for thinking in terms of degrees or extent of racism has merit. Consider the National Basketball Association's 2011 lockout and the media frenzy around ESPN analyst Bryant Gumbel's remarks comparing Commissioner David Stern's approach to that of a "modern plantation overseer." The debate surrounding Gumbel's comparison focused on the question of whether or not Stern is a racist. It was exactly the binary logic to which Rattansi points. If, instead, we accept that racism is a multifaceted hydra that can manifest itself in a variety of ways depending upon historical and cultural factors, then instead of pondering whether or not Stern is racist, the conversation would ask: What elements of the situation at hand might exhibit and embody racist discourse and practice? Because racism can appear in multiple forms, resisting simplistic either-or arguments enables us to discern nuanced manifestations as well as quite overt ones.

Anthony Appiah, in a similar vein, questions the notion of racial identity as constructed in contemporary society. Appiah focuses on the complexity and multiplicity of "identity" as a term that first appeared in the 1950s to suggest that personal identity is shaped by race, ethnicity, gender, religion, nationality, even sexuality.[7] He argues, "Once labels are applied to people, ideas about people who fit the label come to have social and psychological effects."[8] Appiah goes on to suggest a particular threefold structure to collective identities or groups related to features such as race and gender.

First, public discourse requires terms that can label certain identifiable characteristics. While the conceptual boundaries are not precise, the broad category is generally understood. Second, at least some of the people who bear those labels will internalize the category as part of their identity. In this sense, the label may shape a person's feelings, actions, or behavioral norms and, at the same time, will enable the person to locate him- or herself within collective narratives. A person's personal story can be understood as part of a larger story. The third structure to collective or group identities shapes the patterns of behavior toward such labels or the treatment that these labeled or named groups receive. Discrimination can be considered one form of treatment, but behavioral patterns can also take a benevolent form.[9]

Appiah thus demonstrates how race and other dimensions of identity are socially constructed. They are "real" sources of differentiation only in the sense that people will identify themselves or others as belonging to a certain group and act in response to those categorizations. These actions may or may not be consciously enacted. As

Appiah claims, "The contours of identity are profoundly real: and yet no more imperishable, unchanging, or transcendent than other things that men and women make."[10]

One example of the real, yet evolving nature of racial identity within the United States is the decennial census. The racial categories change from census to census in an attempt to better categorize the nation's demographics. For example, in 1990, there were five broad categories for self-identifying one's race: White; Black; American Indian, Eskimo, Aleut; Asian or Pacific Islander; and Other Race. Persons of "Hispanic" origin are both included in those racial categories and then separated out (thus, the well known, "White, Non-Hispanic" category).[11] In 2000 and 2010, the census expanded the categories for racial identity to: White; Black or African American; American Indian and Alaska Native; Asian; Native Hawaiian and Other Pacific Islander; and Some Other Race. Although persons of "Hispanic" origin may choose to iden-tify as white, black, or some other race, persons of African descent or African and European or Anglo descent are expected to select "Black or African American," even though they might appear and live as white people. Meanwhile, "Hispanics" who do not consider themselves white or black simply opt for "some other race," despite the fact that on their birth certificates, many Latinos and Latinas were entered as "white," presumably meaning, "not black." Again, categories of race are fluid, shifting, and socially constructed, yet continue to have a profound influence on the lives of many persons.

Because his analysis focuses on the political realm, Appiah then demonstrates that within the context of a democratic society such as the United States, there has been a post-Enlightenment struggle to extend equivalent treatment to all members of the society, regardless of the other identities that shape them. Equal treatment should be extended by the state not so much to all groups, but to each citizen as citizen no matter his or her group or collective identity. Group status should be nei-ther the source of political and social rights nor the cause for exclusion. To illustrate, Appiah notes: "It was an objection to the membership rights of whites (and the membership burdens of blacks) that underlay much of the opposition to the American Jim Crow and to apartheid."[12] Appiah refers to this standard for the state as *neutrality as equal respect*."[13] Appiah in no way conflates the theoretical democratic ideal with the reality of differential and discriminatory treatment within the United States. Instead, his intention is to consider the theoretical context for identity and to add complexity to much of the current debate.

Adding fuel to the fire, Appiah argues for the meaninglessness of the widely used concept of "culture" as well as "cultural diversity," offering evidence to the effect that, compared to seventy years ago, Americans are increasingly born in the United States, live outside neighborhoods that share their "national" origins, and speak English (despite the sentiment that Spanish is rapidly becoming a second language in America).[14] If such distinctive marks or elements of culture are disappearing, what then does "culture" or "cultural diversity" signify? He further troubles the waters in his analysis of racial identities in the United States by suggesting they often function to undermine the social identity, which may have been intended as a source of strength and solidarity:

> Many Americans believe that a person with one African American and one European American parent is an African American, following the so-called "one-drop rule" that prevailed in some conceptions of black identity. . . . While most Americans understand this to mean that some African Americans will "look white," they mostly suppose that this phenomenon is rare in relation to the African American population as a whole. But in fact, it seems that very many—perhaps even a majority— of the Americans who are descended from African slaves "look white," are treated as white, and identify as such. To put the matter as paradoxically as possible: many people who are African American by the one-drop rule are, are regarded as, and regard themselves as white.[15]

In other words, African Americans may or may not "look" black or white and may or may not "pass" as whites in the society of the United States. Moreover, there may be many "white" persons who have no idea that according to the one-drop rule they are, in fact, African American. Identity, and perhaps above all, racial identity is a theoretically complicated, contested, and elusive subject.

Even as scholars debate the meaning of race, the praxiological reality, the lived expression of countless people, remains racist and racialized, even within the context of a post-civil rights society. Those whom the majority culture would deem "other-than-white" find it difficult to deny the existence of racism, even if class, gender, and other factors play a role in discrimination and the pervasive sense of disadvantage accruing to the logic of race. Yet for white Americans, even white Christian Americans, the notion of racial discrimination often evokes anger and denial accompanied by claims to individual or group culpability for failing to take advantage of existing opportunities extended through legal measures that prohibit discrimination based upon identity. This phenomenon, to which we shall return in chapter 3, is variously referred to as "color-blind racism," "racial realism," and "modern racism."[16] Contemporary racial discourse is marked by a few central assumptions. First, the logic suggests that civil rights legislation was successful and racial inequalities have been eliminated, though some *individual* acts of racism still occur. Second, any policies related to equal and fair treatment are now unnecessary, since the playing field has been leveled. With the first two pieces in place, the third assumption attributes any lack of success within the United States to the failure of racial groups to take advantage of the opportunities that exist. "Cultural" characteristics, as well as a persistent "victim" mentality, are deemed responsible for this failure. While it is true that overt forms of racism such as slavery, Jim Crow laws, and boarding schools for tribal children are a thing of the past, subtle and covert forms of racism embedded in institutional and social practices continue to manifest discriminatory practices in addition to this form of discriminatory rhetoric, as we will explore in chapter 3.

Racism, in sum, is not one practice or form of discourse, but an evolving and re-creating manifestation of the logic of superiority and inferiority, signaled by physical characteristics, but socially located and constructed. It has always been and remains a multifaceted hydra. Racism may take the form of laws, policies, comments and jokes, or subtle or overt practices within institutions. As a result, it cannot be construed as simply a matter of political decree, since economics, power, and religion also influence the shape of racialized discourse and practice. Moreover, silence or neutrality can function to reinforce racist discourse and practice.

White Privilege and White Supremacy

In the past, it has often been the case that whiteness and its position as superior to other-than-whiteness was openly pronounced and practiced. In the twenty-first century, when overt racism is no longer a politically viable option, it takes on varied masks and guises intended to confuse its identification. One of the ways to begin revealing its ongoing presence is to name and expose the benefits accruing to whiteness in the United States. White privilege and white supremacy are little recognized and frequently misunderstood phenomena. Both, as

Cone has pointed out, cause emotional discomfort to white Americans when named and discussed. Perhaps the discomfort provides a vital sign of the need to wrestle with a certain level of moral failure in accepting advantages received merely by means of the possession of "white" skin. In her influential and widely published essay, "White Privilege: Unpacking the Invisible Knapsack," Peggy McIntosh describes white privilege as "an invisible package of unearned assets which I can count on cashing in each day, but about which I was 'meant' to remain oblivious."[17] McIntosh's metaphor of a knapsack on one's back should be supplemented by the image of a set of blinders that restricts white Americans' vision. Not only do white people have an unearned set of advantages upon which they can draw, these advantages often remain unseen, unrecognized, and unacknowledged. McIntosh lists twenty-six examples of white privilege, such as: "I can if I wish arrange to be in the company of people of my race most of the time"; "I am never asked to speak for all people of my racial group"; and "I can choose blemish cover or bandages in 'flesh' color and have them more or less match my skin."[18] One additional example, phrased somewhat differently from McIntosh's statement, is of particular note in the context of this argument and the historical analysis to follow: White Americans can expect that white history will be routinely taught in the public school system and not as a special month, week, or day. And graduate students in the humanities and social sciences who are white will not be required to master two bodies of literature if they wish to include the contributions of their own race. McIntosh's essay is exemplary in illuminating the movement from understanding one's own marginalization—in this case, a feminist who experienced the discriminatory reality of patriarchal systems—to a conscientization of the ways in which one's own social location, in turn, can be privileged in relationship to others.

Adding to McIntosh's argument of unearned advantages is the generally unacknowledged normativity of whiteness within the United States. Steve Garner argues that, "Because of the dominance of Western European thought and military and technological power over the last five centuries in its global projects of colonialism and neo-colonialism, whiteness has come to be *represented* as humanness, normality, and universality."[19] Thus, concludes Garner, whiteness is not invisible; to the contrary, it is "unmarked" in the sense that many white people do not even understand themselves to be identified with a race. Acknowledging white privilege, the sense of white as normative and even nonracial, often results in discursive claims that will deflect "attention from whiteness as a privilege-holding social location."[20] Turning to questions of reverse discrimination or arguing that we now live in a color-blind society represent two of these discursive escape hatches. Nevertheless, the creation of whiteness and its privileges has been a function of Anglo and European American theory, science, and practice across centuries. It is a function of human agency not a random, natural, or divinely sanctioned reality.

Closely related to white privilege is the reality of white supremacy, which is often positioned as a reference to extremist groups such as the Ku Klux Klan. However, by definition, white supremacy refers to white cultural domination within the context of the United States. Philosopher Charles Mills notes, "Unlike the currently more fashionable 'white privilege,' *white supremacy* implies the existence of a system that not only privileges whites but is run by whites, for white benefit."[21] Mills goes on to say that using the term "white supremacy" shifts the discourse from its focus on individuals and intentions to systems and power. White supremacy brings to the forefront questions of power, not only the power to create and sustain a system that advantages white people, but the power to reinscribe and reinvent the system in response to changing legal and social dynamics and realities. In this way, white people need not even hold the numerical majority within a society; they need only continually recreate the system that privileges whiteness. Clearly, this was the case for many years in South Africa. It can also be seen, for example, in a state such as Texas where the majority culture might be Latino/a, but the school board continues to circumscribe the curriculum in order to teach the history of white dominance, superiority, and culture as normative.

We must be clear that this argument is not intended to suggest that white privilege and white supremacy actually mean the white race is superior or, by virtue of the systemic sin inherent in white supremacy, the white race is actually fatally flawed and evil. God did not create races; societies have. What it does mean is that continued participation in systemic sin is morally reprehensible and untenable from a Christian perspective. A conscientization process is required, in which white Americans grasp the reality of white privilege and white supremacy and discern their incompatibility with the gospel of Jesus Christ. Moreover, consciousness of the privileged position of whiteness then requires a form of repentance that leads to dismantling racist systems and structures. Having established this theoretical and sociological background or framework offering insights into the nature of racism, it is now possible to examine the relationship of Christian discourse and practice to the logic, practices, and persistence of racism.

Constantinian versus Prophetic Christianity

Any attempt to describe "Christian discourse and practice" is laced with theoretical and practical obstacles. The multiplicities of Christian discourse and practice vary according to the historical era, geographical location, social location, and a host of other interpretive realities. There is no singular "Christianity" at a thick level of analysis. The earliest Christian discourse and practice, as expressed in the Jesus movement, was radically reshaped and redirected under Constantine the Great, Roman emperor from 307 to 337, who made Christianity the religion of the state. No longer subject to persecution, Christianity took on favored status. Evidence suggests Constantine embraced some aspects of Christian faith and acted according to those beliefs, though it is also the case that Christianity enabled him to consolidate power and reinforce his position. It was a strategic move for Constantine, as much as a one based on faith. On this point of mixed motives, theologian Joerg Rieger argues that the Eusebius account of Constantine's conversion demonstrates "[r]eligious and political concerns cannot be separated. . . . Consequently, those who see religion and politics as separate realms have to doubt the sincerity of Constantine's conversion."[22]

Nevertheless, the consolidation of Christian religion, as it joins forces with social, political, and economic concerns, is how Latin American theologian Enrique Dussel defines "Christendom." Christianity, according to Dussel, is a religion; "'Christendom' is a cultural reality."[23] Christendom under Constantine "was a mixture of Christian and Hellenistic elements. It was a political unity."[24] Dussel then goes on to suggest it was also an economic unity, not simply an ecclesiastical or political one. Thus, as early as the fourth century, Christianity began to intertwine with politics, economics, and power, but under the rubric of the sovereignty of God. As Rieger notes, Constantine's theology would have held that the one God rules over everything, whether religion or politics or any other aspect of the Roman Empire.[25] Notably, race does not yet seem to be a central feature of Christendom, though to sustain political and economic power racism will become inextricably linked to Christian religion in the

West, especially in the United States. Like Constantine's Christianity, white Americans have used Christianity to consolidate power and reinforce privilege vis-à-vis persons of color. Subsequent chapters will begin to unravel and expose the theological relationship of racism to politics, economics, and power.

In his book *Democracy Matters*, Cornel West continues his quest to unveil "the ways in which the vicious legacy of white supremacy contributes to the arrested development of American democracy."[26] He argues that "race is the crucial intersecting point where democratic energies clash with American imperial realities" and Manifest Destiny provides the fulcrum for discriminatory practices.[27] The racialized logic of American society from the beginning enabled the construction of the democratic, capitalist nation we inhabit today. West writes, "The most painful truth in the making of America—a truth that shatters all pretensions to innocence and undercuts all efforts of denial—is that *the enslavement of Africans and the imperial expansion over indigenous peoples and their lands were undeniable preconditions for the possibility of American democracy*."[28] This configuration represents the American version of Constantinian Christianity, especially having been formulated under the justifying rationale of the will of God.

At the risk of oversimplifying West's argument, Constantinian Christianity co-opts the message of Christian faith as it becomes intertwined with state power for purposes of maintaining that power and fulfilling self-interest. It thus acquires an authoritarian character that is at risk of supporting imperial ends. In the United States, Constantinian Christianity also emphasizes "personal conversion, individual piety, and philanthropic service [but] has lost its fervor for the suspicion of worldly authorities and for doing justice in the service of the most vulnerable among us."[29] In other words, Constantinian Christianity thwarts attempts to expose systemic sin and undermine its privileged position. Prophetic Christianity, in contrast, refers to the tradition arising out of the Jewish prophets and extending into the ministry of Jesus in which justice and compassion are central and the worship of "the idol of human power" is rejected.[30] The idol of material wealth is also critiqued by prophetic Christianity, which places "a premium on the kind of human being one chooses to be rather than the amount of commodities one possesses."[31] Although Constantinian Christianity has often dominated life in the United States, West is careful to point out prophetic tendencies as well that have furthered the democratic impulses of the nation and provided greater freedoms to those who have been trampled underfoot by the logic of Manifest Destiny. In the United States, Christianity has never lost an undercurrent of the prophetic faith of the Jesus movement. Theologically, both expressions of Christianity are bound to persist this side of the new creation, but the demand of the gospel to speak truth to power suggests Constantinian Christianity must be continually interrogated.

Supplementing West's differentiation between Constantinian and Prophetic trajectories of Christianity is Rieger's analysis of top-down versus bottom-up power. Power, of course, is an indispensable component in racist discourse and practice. Rieger argues that the Roman Empire provides an example of the top-down paradigm, in which power and wealth are concentrated "in the hands of a few, to the detriment of the majority of people."[32] The Jesus movement came into conflict with Rome precisely because it followed the opposite logic. Rieger surmises that "at the heart of these conflicts was the question of power and its theological justification: Was divine power located at the top, with the various elites, or was divine power at work at the bottom, with the people—where the Jesus movement kept building?"[33] Although the rulers may demonstrate a level of tolerance toward the power from below, their elite position requires the maintenance of structures, policies, and public discourse in order to limit and circumscribe those at the bottom of the system. Even in a democracy, this dynamic of top down versus bottom up power persists.

Whether framed in the terms of Dussel, West, or Rieger, the pattern is clear. Within a few centuries of the emergence of the Jesus movement, Christian religion was related to politics, economics, and power—a trajectory that has continued in various manifestations. Christian discourse and practice can be an instrument to secure and further the interests of a particular group, class, or people who wield a level of power and wealth that, in turn, can limit the power and wealth of those who are not among the ruling or elite members of the society.[34] Yet, the early Christian movement up to the time of Constantine and in various manifestations throughout history has pursued a different logic of faith, one that places justice, compassion, and the flourishing of life for all persons at the forefront. Though critics may argue that Dussel, West, and Rieger all represent a particular theological perspective, it is hard for all but the most skeptical to deny that, in large measure, the Christianity existing in the United States often resembles Constantinian Christianity more than it does the prophetic Jesus movement. This is why radical movements such as Shane Claiborne's "The Simple Way" evoke such widespread interest. Hence, these choices—the top-down power of Constantinian Christianity or the bottom-up power of Prophetic Christianity or the Jesus movement—underlie and shape the formation, continuation, and potential dismantling of racism in the United States. Constantinian Christianity and Prophetic Christianity approach the doctrine of theological anthropology with radically different assumptions, interpretations, and objectives.

In the next chapter, we explore how race and racism influence the construction and articulation of theological anthropology, in order to grasp the ongoing presence of racist and racialized discourse and practice in theology.

2

BEING HUMAN

That which the racist glorifies in himself is his being. And that which he scorns and rejects in members of out-races is precisely their human being.

—George D. Kelsey

Though most Hispanic women suffer racial/ethnic and sexist oppression and most of us also suffer poverty, we do not go about our vida cotidiana—our everyday life—thinking that we suffer but rather thinking how to struggle to survive, to live fully.

—Ada María Isasi-Díaz

When a society's priorities are redirected radically to alleviating the majority of its members' plight through phasing out the super-elite's privileges, genuine democracy results. In the reconfiguration of an obsessively racialized society, we develop both collective selves and unique individuality. In this way, all people enjoy the grace of possibilities inherent in full human potential.

—Dwight N. Hopkins

From a theological perspective, discussions of racism are inextricably bound to questions of theological anthropology.[1] More precisely, at stake is the question and furtherance of fully human existence. What does it mean to be created in the image of God? What does it mean to be fully human as revealed in Jesus of Nazareth who is the Christ? What does it mean to be sinful yet graced creatures with the potential to become fully human as God created us to be? Persons of color readily recognize the significance of theological anthropology and the struggle for fully human existence, even as racialized expressions of this doctrine escape the consciousness of many, perhaps most, white theologians.

James Cone and Fully Human Existence

James Cone, the originator of liberation theologies in the context of the United States, recognized from the outset that theological anthropology was, perhaps, the central question for African Americans in light of the gospel of Jesus Christ. Even as Cone maintains a firm christological center for his theology, he begins *Black Theology and Black Power* (1969) by defining the Black Power movement in terms of the affirmation of the humanity of black Americans. Cone argues that "white historians and political scientists have attempted, perhaps subconsciously, to camouflage the inhumanity of whites toward blacks. But the evidence is clear . . . all aspects of this society have participated in the act of enslaving blacks, extinguishing Indians, and annihilating all who question white society's right to decide who is human."[2] Cone raises the pivotal question of the day, asking "How should I respond to a world which defines me as a nonperson?"[3]

Although *Black Theology* and *Black Power* explicitly examined the Triune God and ecclesiology in relation to Black Power, the question of fully human existence remained central to the construction of each doctrine and interwoven through each chapter. First, Cone suggests that theological anthropology has been constructed from a white theological perspective that lacks meaning for the black community:

> The [New Testament] message is presented to blacks as if they shared the white cultural tradition. We still talk of salvation in white terms, love with a Western perspective, and thus never ask the question, What are the theological implications of God's love for the black [person] in America? Therefore when we are confronted with blacks with a new sense of themselves, alien to the Western definition of the black [person] and, to some degree, even alien to the Western view of humanity, our language seems to fail us as an attempt is made to "fit him in."[4]

Cone rightly suggests that under conditions of oppression, any definition of fully human existence will be suspect in the eyes of those struggling for freedom and dignity if that concept is constructed by those who benefit from and uphold the systemic advantages of the society. If white theology either diminishes the humanity of persons of color or remains silent with regard to their dehumanization, then can this message be considered consistent with the gospel of Jesus Christ?

Cone approaches the doctrine positively later in the same chapter. Blackness is constructed as a "special creation of God" and this "means that God has bestowed" on black Americans a new image of themselves, "so that [they] can now become what [they] in fact [are]."⁵ Fully human existence not only means accepting that black persons are created in the image of God and given a "new image of [themselves] revealed in Jesus Christ" but also that African Americans love themselves in a society that has despised and demeaned them.⁶ Fully human existence is thereby an act of divine grace received by means of self-love or self-affirmation. Cone further asserts that as a new creature in Christ, the black American is called to fully human existence, despite the white society's attempt to undermine the goodness, love, and righteousness of God. Yet, for Cone, it is more than a matter of theological discourse, as action must conform to rhetoric: "It seems that the mistake of most whites . . . is their insistence on telling blacks how to respond 'as Christians' to racism, insisting that nonviolence is the only appropriate response. But there is an ugly contrast between the sweet, nonviolent language of white Christians and their participation in a violently unjust system."⁷ We should not miss the significance of Cone's early attempt to highlight systemic sin and institutional racism as theologically relevant considerations.

Further, Cone's theological anthropology is not simply about fully human existence for black Americans; it is equally about the full humanity of white persons. It is about fully human existence, not from a universal perspective, but as a contextually and socially located reality in relation to the divine. Cone repeatedly articulates that freedom in Christ for the oppressed is freedom also for the oppressor: "Christ in liberating the wretched of the earth also liberates those responsible for the wretchedness. The oppressor is also freed of his peculiar demons. Black Power shouting Yes to black humanness and No to white oppression is exorcizing demons on both sides of the conflict."⁸ In other words, those who create and sustain racist discourse and practices also need to be liberated in order to be fully human as God created them to be.

In Cone's *The Cross and the Lynching Tree*, written over forty years after the publication of *Black Theology and Black Power*, the question of fully human existence continues to provide a backdrop to his theological argument. He acknowledges that, "The struggle to make sense of being *black* and *Christian* in white America has motivated all my work as a theologian, starting in June 1968, two months after Martin King's assassination, when I began to write *Black Theology and Black Power*."⁹

31

In 2011, Cone takes up a taboo subject, lynching, and the christological implications of this heinous crime, as he draws comparisons of lynched black bodies to the crucifixion of Jesus Christ. Once again, in powerful theological terms, Cone carries forward his project to resist white supremacy, "to affirm black humanity, and to defend it."[10] Moreover, Cone's objective remains the conscientization of both black and white America, so that the great systemic sin of racism, of white supremacy in the United States, might finally be healed by the power of the cross. Although Cone is the progenitor of liberation theologies in the United States, the centrality of theological anthropology has been a pervasive and recurring theme in the work of scholars of color.

Naming Racism, Reconstructing Theological Anthropology

Recent book-length studies by theologians of color demonstrate the centrality of theological anthropology and the identification of race, despite and because of its ambiguous and socially constructed nature. Rubén Rosario Rodríguez's *Racism and God-Talk*, Miguel H. Díaz's *On Being Human*, and Dwight Hopkins's *Being Human*, help to illustrate the centrality of theological anthropology in relation to the racialized context of theology and the church. Rodríguez acknowledges that he understands the role of racism on an experiential level, having lived as a Latino Christian in the United States. His goal is to help make transparent the ways theology and the church have been implicated in the country's racial history and to offer a constructive alternative theological approach rooted and grounded in a more complete articulation of human beings in relation to the divine. On a theological and ecclesiastical level, the affirmation of fully human existence necessarily remains a work in progress, as theological discourse is, by nature, provisional and incomplete. For Rodríguez, racist history has emphasized the black-white conversation but needs to be expanded to include others who have suffered within the white European and Anglo dominated culture of the United States and under the racism that pervades the church as well as society. Rodríguez argues for the persistence of systemic sin within the church:

There is no universally accepted Christian confessional statement that confronts the problem of racism by affirming the full humanity of all persons as *imago Dei* regardless of national origin or differences in physical appearance. While all the major Christian denominations in the United States have adopted language and policies denouncing racism since the advent of the civil rights movement, Christian doctrines of humanity—in their analysis of the human condition—have largely ignored the role of racial prejudice in perpetuating sinful social conditions.[11]

In an attempt to break open racist discourse and practices, Rodríguez introduces the concept of *mestizaje*, "mutual exchange between two or more cultures," which provides language to name and discuss a phenomenon that "has always been a vital part of the Christian tradition."[12] He then reconstructs Christian doctrines through the lens of *mestizaje*, demonstrating its function as "a set of communal practices distinguished by a moral choice to recognize the inherent dignity of all human beings."[13] Ultimately, Rodríguez argues that the intersection and mutual sharing of different cultural traditions and strands of Christianity can cultivate a greater ecumenicity and a more just church and society in which all may express their full humanity. Unfortunately, despite his attempt to expand and deepen the meaning of human being, it is likely that some, perhaps many white theologians regard Rodríguez's book and proposal as marginal or peripheral to the core theological tradition precisely because of its location and particularity as a Latino/a local theology. In other words, it is viewed as a book largely for Latino/as.

In his study from a Catholic theological perspective, Miguel Díaz approaches theological anthropology through a "U.S. Hispanic" lens that reconstructs fully human existence in conversation with the writings of Karl Rahner.[14] He asserts that, "U.S. Hispanic theological anthropology can be systematically, philosophically, and theologically enriched by engaging in an explicit conversation with Karl Rahner, and Karl Rahner's theological anthropology can be deepened, developed, and critiqued from the perspective of U.S. Hispanic visions."[15] Much of Díaz's conversation with Rahnerian theology is intended to demonstrate the continuity of Hispanic theology with the core Catholic theological tradition while expanding Rahner's trajectory toward the social, communal, and contextual character of theology as well as the increasingly global nature of the church.

Hence, Díaz is concerned to develop a theological understanding of being "Hispanically human" as a "socially constituted subject" in relationship to the divine.[16] To be Hispanic in the context of the United States relates to a common language that "speaks specific human identity" into being.[17] It is a manifestation of one's humanity located within a community. To be human is also related to the concept of *mestizaje* or *mulatez*, the comingling of races, cultures, and ethnicities so as to create a sense of "living 'in-between' two worlds."[18] This reality, of course, will undoubtedly become more prominent within the population of the United States and further complicates attempts at racial categorization. *Mestizaje* also means that to be Hispanically human is to experience forms of exile and marginalization.[19]

Following a survey of major Latino and Latina theologians, Díaz summarizes the contours of being Hispanically human articulated therein. He emphasizes that, "concrete historical experiences become essential in defining who people are and who they become as they encounter and respond to grace *within their history*"[20] Rather than denying the lived reality of various peoples, Latino and Latina theologians argue that historical and social locations are exactly the places where grace is encountered and are, therefore, integral to understanding fully human existence. We are not creatures who live in the abstract, but ones who encounter God within particular and concrete contexts. Theological discourse that fails to recognize the concrete locations of the encounter with grace also denies or obscures the in-breaking divine reality.

As Díaz places this understanding of being Hispanically human in conversation with Rahner's theology, two points emerge that deserve consideration. First, Díaz demonstrates that the recognition of race, ethnicity, or other particular contextual realities is not incompatible with more traditional white male theologies (and vice versa). In fact, these theological perspectives serve to deepen and enrich one another, thus better attesting to the divine relationship to humanity. It is, in a sense, theological *mestizaje*. Second, he provides evidence that theological methods other than strictly liberation methods can attend to questions of race.[21] Indeed, if this is the case, then racialized discourse should not be limited to liberation theologies proper, but challenge all theological methods to engage the particularities of human being.

Dwight Hopkins's *Being Human* attempts to construct a theological anthropology, "from a black theology vantage point not only because conceptual clarity demands such a move. The practical urgency of creating an alternative vision of what humans in the United States and, indeed, the world human community can become also compels us to attempt a liberating theological anthropology."[22] Hopkins argues that the social construction of "race presents, perhaps, the superlative overarching mark of what a human being is in the United States."[23] As such, a constructive theological anthropology "necessitates a theoretical and historical engagement with race."[24] But Hopkins' argument goes one step further in suggesting that, in the context of the United States, a "spirituality of white supremacy" must be dismantled. If spirituality is denoted as that which brings meaning to the lives of people and communities, this demonic spirituality weaves together socially-constructed notions of race and concepts of beauty, reinforced and maintained by the exercise of power (or lack thereof). "Consequently, to be sane in America," concludes Hopkins, "is to simply agree that white people's perpetual position at the top of the racial hierarchy is normal. Of course only the mad would dispute this normative assertion."[25] In the end, *Being Human* presents a forceful case that any contemporary theological anthropology requires the prior step of analyzing race alongside culture and concepts of the self or selves. Unfortunately, few theologies take seriously the importance of racialized discourse and practice. Again, white supremacy has the power, under the guise of neutrality, to position Hopkins's argument as marginal, directed at African Americans, but not central to the larger theological tradition.

Women of color have been equally adept at illuminating racialized dimensions of theology while highlighting interlocking issues of gender and class, often deepening the understanding of the interplay of race with other social, political, and economic factors. In the introductory chapter to *Deeper Shades of Purple*, a collection of significant womanist theological voices and influences, Stacey Floyd-Thomas demonstrates the centrality of fully human existence to their constructive project: "What characterizes womanist discourse is that Black women are engaged in the process of knowledge production that is most necessary for their own flourishing rather than being exploited for the enlightenment and entertainment of white psyches and male egos."[26] The essays throughout the volume attend to the meaning of fully human existence in a racist and patriarchal society.

Contributor Diana Hayes, for example, writes that, "Part of my struggle is to name and affirm myself and my sisters as women of African descent who have been denied their rightful place in the history of humanity." But, in a manner reminiscent of Cone, Hayes also emphasizes that, "I believe that my rights as an African American, as a Black woman, are guaranteed only when the rights of all people are guaranteed; . . . that my human dignity and thus my creation in God is denied when that of others is trampled into the dirt for any reason."[27] This refrain is reiterated when Cheryl Kirk-Duggan writes, "In hope and transformation, a *Womanist* emancipator theory engenders mutuality and community amid the responsibility and stewardship of freedom, and honors the *imago Dei*, the image of God—the essential goodness within all persons."[28] The idea represented by these and other womanists pushes against the binary logic of oppressed and oppressor, as well as polarized arguments that elevate one group at the expense of others. Such considerations do not excuse racist discourse and practice. Rather, they illuminate the complexity and multiplicity of oppressions that exist in the society. Womanists deepen the conversation as they demonstrate that fully human existence is often undermined by a number of interlocking systems that layer and interweave discriminatory patterns and logic.

Significantly, the drive toward fully human existence identifies religious discourse and practice as a key component of resisting dehumanizing forces. Indeed, Rosemarie Freeney Harding names what so many people of color have experienced in spite of racism; the sense that religion—in this case as embodied in African American communities in the South—is *"that which keeps us human in the world."*[29] Harding does not mean religion as an organized cultural artifact, but as a relationship with the divine, as a spiritual reality. Here the distinction Dussel makes between Christianity and Christendom or West's Constantinian versus Prophetic Christianity might be applicable. To be human is to live in light of the divine Other, despite the injustice and corruption of the society. Paradoxically, within black communities, the religion that facilitated the humanity of the people was the one same religion that sought to dehumanize them. Fundamental to theological anthropologies constructed by persons of color is this paradoxical reality and the claiming of religious truth in defiance of the cultural co-optation of the Christian faith. The challenging of knowledge, the claiming of human agency, the affirmation of one's own humanity created in the image of God are essential dimensions of womanist approaches to theological anthropology.

This notion of fully human existence as undermined and limited by racist discourse and practice is central to the theological anthropology of Latinas as well. In "Who is Americana/o," Michelle Gonzalez begins her essay by stating what should be the obvious, but is too seldom acknowledged: "In modern history, this area [theological anthropology] (and theology in general) has been elaborated predominantly through the lens of European and Euro-American philosophers and theologians, with a heavy emphasis on the individual."[30] The Enlightenment and modern concept of the autonomous self figures prominently in racist logic, and as we shall observe in chapter 3, continues to hold sway on the contemporary articulation of color-blind racism, ascribing lack of success to individual failure. While arguing for the "porous" nature of human identity as represented in theories of hybridity and realities of historical colonialism in conversation with Latina and Latino theological anthropologies, Gonzalez concludes that the *mestizo/a* and *mulato/a* identities in the United States challenge Euro-centric representations of human being, not only in undermining racial and ethnic categorizations but also in subverting the emphasis on individualism over deeper communal expressions. Gonzalez challenges white theologians to explore typically unexamined assumptions. In particular, the communal nature of Christian faith necessarily rejects the exercise of enlightened individualism at the expense of one's neighbor.

Mujerista theologian Ada María Isasi-Díaz is among the earliest and most influential Latina theologians. Her book, *Mujerista Theology*, investigates particular "modes of oppression" suffered by Latinas.[31] Central to the discussion is the notion that oppression impedes individuals' and communities' ability to develop their potential and to pursue fully human existence. Mujerista theology begins with the claim that the impulse of what we are identifying as "Constantinian Christianity" or "Christendom" has been toward marginalizing, silencing, and oppressing Latinas. As such, fully human existence is located first in self-determination and *la lucha*, the struggle for justice against five primary modes of oppression: exploitation, marginalization, powerlessness, cultural imperialism, and systemic violence. Of note is the oppressive mode of cultural imperialism, which Isasi-Díaz defines as "the very basis for ethnic prejudice and racism."[32] Accordingly, it is not simply a matter of what this cultural imperialism "does to Latinas but what it makes Latinas do to our own selves. Little by little we internalize the way the dominant culture sees us."[33] The power of the majority culture to shape knowledge and normativity, as Michel Foucault notably theorized, masks the insidious nature of racist discourse and practice.

Thus, Isasi-Díaz constructs her theological anthropology in response to the oppressive modes that dehumanize Latinas, in particular. Her understanding of fully human existence arising out of the oppression of Latinas is located in three ways of articulating the reality of their lives.

First, the struggle (*la lucha*); second, allow me to speak (*permítanme hablar*); and third, the community and the family (*la communidad/la familia*).[34] In addition to the notion of the struggle articulated above, the question of being allowed to speak and speak for themselves, on their own terms, is of central concern. It enables Latinas to be "protagonists" in their own history, to interrupt the internalized narratives of the majority culture, and "to become full moral agents, full persons in [their] own right."[35] Reminiscent of Gonzalez's assertion, the third reality of Latinas' lives pushes back against the individualism, the autonomous self of the majority culture, and upholds the interrelationships that characterize their cultural norms. In sum, for Isasi-Díaz, theological anthropology "is not about an idealized type of humanity or about an abstract understanding of humanity," but about a deep awareness of their context as essential to articulating the fullness of what it means to be human and created in the image of God.[36]

Asian theologians likewise express concern for dismantling racist discourse and practice. Andrew Sung Park's *The Wounded Heart of God* draws upon the cultural concept of "han" in delineating a theological anthropology aimed at fully human existence. Although born in Korea, Park's experience growing up in the United States brings together these two perspectives as he addresses suffering within the East Asian context. Park defines *han* as "the critical wound of the heart generated by unjust psychosomatic repression, as well as by social, political, economic, and cultural oppression. It is entrenched in the hearts of the victims of sin and violence, and is expressed through such diverse reactions as sadness, helplessness, hopelessness, resentment, hatred, and the will to revenge."[37] Fully human existence therefore requires not only attention to sin and human agency, but also to the victims of sin and suffering and the trauma that accompanies this wounded heart.

Han provides the conceptual basis for how race and racism are addressed within Park's theological anthropology. Emphasizing the collective experience of *han* located in groups of people, *han* at the collective, unconscious level can be expressed as "racial mourning" arising from generations of oppression, injustice, and exploitation.[38] In its active form, collective unconscious *han* leads to racial resentment; in its passive form, "the ethos of racial lamentation." The former is closely associated with long-term antagonisms that may erupt in violence. The latter is a deep anguish that finds expression in artistic forms.[39] Beyond this collective human experience, Park notes that *han* can also manifest itself within animals and nature through continual degradation and abuse by human beings. Ultimately, like sin, *han* must find resolution in and through God, beginning with a conscientization process.

Park's analysis of fully human existence as limited by *han* is not argued solely through a Korean lens. Instead, he weaves in the experiences of various peoples as illustrative. African American spirituals and the blues illustrate an expression of passive unconscious collective *han*. Feminist theology assists in his reconstruction of Western notions of sin and salvation. References to traditional white theologians, as well as those of scholars of color provide for an integrative understanding of fully human existence, as the common experience of *han* is discerned in various contexts.

Native American theological anthropology likewise interrogates white, Western perspectives on fully human existence and the meaning of being human through a unique lens and world view. Native Americans incorporate a traditional understanding of all living things as "people." Human beings represent only one type of people, such that the whole of creation is revered as every created thing is included among "all my relations" who deserve dignity and respect. In *A Native American Theology*, collaborators Clara Sue Kidwell, Homer Noley, and George E. Tinker approach traditional Christian doctrines through the lens of Native American spirituality, culture, and history.

Chapter 5, entitled "Theological Anthropology," arguably delineates an anthropological account more so than an explicitly theological exploration of human being. Yet, at the outset, the authors shift the traditional theological category and questions as they contend:

> Theological anthropology is concerned with defining the human person as a religious being. For Native Americans, their intimate relationship with the natural environment blurs the distinctions between human and non-human. Human beings are not the only people in the world. . . . We must move beyond the Christian tradition of humans as unique creations of God to the idea that the world of persons is all embracing.[40]

As a result of this holistic perspective, their theological anthropology steers toward a recognition of the violence done by the majority culture not only to Native peoples but also to the other peoples who populate the earth, including animals, fish, trees, rivers, and even minerals and the land itself. It challenges the notion of the human being as the superior being and thereby challenges racist discourse and practice, given the radical relationality of the whole of creation.

Throughout the volume, the authors emphasize this alternative framework that exists among First Peoples, which calls into question Western epistemological norms. In addition to the interrelatedness of all of creation, the lack of gender hierarchies that was characteristic of Native communities prior to the introduction of Western patriarchy by Christian missionaries, demonstrates a reciprocity that undermines binary dualisms of superior and inferior. A very different notion of fully human existence emerges, but one that has been thwarted over the past four centuries as a result of colonization, acculturation, and annihilation. It is not illegitimate to suggest that, in some ways, Native American traditional values more accurately express the teachings of the early Jesus movement than do the theological doctrines of Constantinian Christianity. Of course, First Peoples resist the colonizers' narrative in maintaining that God or Great Spirit was known to them prior to the arrival of white missionaries. Native Americans, like other theologians of color, recognize the dehumanizing effect of white theological anthropologies and seek to reconstruct the doctrine to facilitate fully human existence for all persons (i.e., the whole of creation).

As a capstone to this consideration of the centrality of racialized discourse and practice to the theological anthropologies written by theologians of color, we turn to two introductory textbooks, *We Have Been Believers* by James Evans Jr. and *Mañana* by Justo González. Evans's chapter on theological anthropology, "On Being Black," explicitly addresses racism. Indeed, Evans suggests that the history of racism forces persons of color to attend to race in theological discourse:

> People of African descent in Europe and North America have not been able to address the question of what it means to be human without, first, wrestling with what it means to be black. One could argue that the question of being black was separated from the question of being human by the elevation of the factor of race to a normative status in relation to the human being.[41]

Pressing back against stereotypical renderings of persons of color and scientific attempts to create racial hierarchies, Evans highlights the seminal work of George Kelsey to demonstrate "the profound, fundamental, basic, essential, fideistic character of racism . . . [that] affects almost every aspect of human existence for African Americans."[42] In other words, meaningful discourse about fully human existence simply cannot sidestep the harsh history and ongoing realities of race. He concludes that an in-depth treatment of theological anthropology from the perspective of black Americans must address "the quest for identity," "the status of African Americans as creations of God," "the Fall in relation to the alienation of black people," and redemption related to "the totality of the human person," not simply rational or moral capacity.[43] Evans's introductory theology text is written from an explicitly African American context, but consciously and intentionally so. In contrast, as we will articulate subsequently, introductory textbooks by white theologians are also socially, culturally, and racially located, but often without acknowledgment of that fact.

In *Mañana*, González begins by acknowledging the contextualized nature of the theological enterprise, stating that, "every theological perspective, no matter how seemingly objective, betrays a bias of which the theologian is not usually aware."[44] He goes on to argue that no abstract theology is possible, but that when we bring our unique experiences, histories, and perspectives to the theological task, it may "help the entire [Christian] community to discover dimensions that have gone unseen."[45] Relating his own story of moving to the United States and becoming part of a minority group, he illustrates how this experience awakened him to the oppression that exists within the society.

His chapter on being human establishes the nature of hierarchies within human life, beginning with the privileging of spirit over body, despite the fact that scripture speaks of the human being as a unity. He next argues that the "hierarchization of body and soul has also led to a devaluation of our relationship to the earth."[46] This ordering and valuing of life is also present among human beings, and although González illustrates this hierarchy in terms of male and female, he clearly notes that "any subjection of a human being to another" dehumanizes both.[47] Although his chapter on theological anthropology does not explicitly address racism, the whole of the chapter is framed in terms of oppression and domination that limit fully human existence and are incompatible with the scriptural witnesses, within a text that is explicitly, though not exclusively, contextualized.

Theologians of color, across the landscape of the last forty years, have interrogated in virtual unanimity racist discourse and practice and articulated theological anthropologies that decenter the normativity of white Western assumptions and epistemology. Given the experience of dehumanization and often the internalization of the logic of oppression, they construct the meaning of human being by deconstructing the racist discourse and practice centered in whiteness and reconstructing the humanity of all peoples as created in the image of God. Their theologies are indebted to both scripture and tradition, but begin with the profound recognition and identification of the dehumanizing conditions experienced by countless people and often in the name of God. They begin with experiences of oppression and marginalization, naming that which undermines the goodness of God and the gospel of abundant life. They speak truth to power. Despite the consistency and unanimity of these voices in regard to the importance of naming the reality of racism in theology and demonstrating how racialized discourse and practice functions to uncover, analyze, and dismantle white privilege and white supremacy, few white theologians today include or address these concerns.

White Theologians' Reticence on Race

Unlike theologians of color, contemporary white theologians have tended to say little on the subject of racism in relation to conceptualizations of theological anthropology. They have little to say on the idea that, in the context of the United States, human categorizations of persons of color embedded in theological constructions and ecclesial practices have diminished countless human lives and contravened the gospel's message of life abundant for those who profess faith in Jesus Christ. They have little to say on the notion that the incorporation of the experiences of non-majority culture people will enable the articulation of a more complete and truthful understanding of fully human existence in relation to the divine. A brief and incomplete, though representative, sampling of white theologians on theological anthropology provides preliminary support for this claim. The intention is not to suggest these theologies are wholly inadequate—indeed, they offer many significant insights into the human condition and relationship to God. However, by illustrating the lack of dialogue with theologians of color, we can demonstrate that white theologians are subject to the same charge they have often forwarded in critique of liberation or contextual theologies: they are limited and too embedded in experiential, localized theological discourse. Indeed, white theologians, writing from the fulcrum of constructed normativity but under the guise of neutrality, find it difficult to listen to and learn from theologians of color.

Admittedly, a few white theologians have attempted anthropologies that do acknowledge and take seriously the racist discourse and practice that remains an ongoing thread woven into the national and ecclesial narratives. When James Cone first published *Black Theology and Black Power*, several white theologians took the challenge seriously and offered preliminary responses. In the first edition of *Black Theology: A Documentary History*, editors Gayraud Wilmore and Cone devoted a section to white responses to black theology, almost as if a sign of hope that genuine dialogue had been initiated.[48] These responses to black theology came from Paul Lehmann, John Bennett, Paul Holmer, and G. Clarke Chapman.[49] Many of these theologians viewed black theology as a potential corrective to and conversation partner with white theology. They responded to Cone with both appreciation and critique. But, in large measure, even those who initially took the question of race quite seriously ultimately proved unable or unwilling to incorporate Cone's theological challenge to white supremacy into their own theology. Granted, the newness of the liberation method combined with the heightened activism of the 1960s and 1970s created a difficult situation and uncharted territory for white theologians to grasp how black theology might inform and transform white theology. Appropriately, many of these white theologians questioned whether a response to black theology was even possible by a white person, given Cone's assertion that white theology needed to remain silent and to listen. Yet, in large measure, any recognition of systemic sin on the part of these white theologians was absent. A case in point is Bennett's contention that "many whites are first- or second-generation Americans and their ancestors had no part in the slave system or in the establishment and hardening of the institutions of discrimination and segregation . . . and they are not won to the black cause by rhetoric that associates them with those sins of American history."[50] Perhaps it was sufficient in that initial phase for white theologians simply to become conscious of black theology's questions and critique of the theological and ecclesial establishment. Conscientization takes time and deliberate engagement, as with any formative process.

Beyond those first attempts to consider racism, race, and racialized discourse as a theological concern, there have been a handful of white theologians in the United States who have sought to take seriously the concerns of theologians of color who struggle to dismantle systemic forces of oppression and dehumanization. Theologians Frederick Herzog, Peter Hodgson, and more recently, James Perkinson represent those who have given explicit attention to racialized discourse and practices within their theological projects as they seek to dismantle racism in theology, the church, and society. Given the long careers and multiple publications of both Herzog and Hodgson, analyzing their theological anthropologies illustrates well the difficulties of entering into racialized discourse and practice.

Herzog's liberation project began in the 1970s and continued until his death in 1995. To his credit, Herzog was already at work on a theology of liberation when Cone's *Black Theology and Black Power* deepened and challenged his thinking. Indeed, in Herzog one can discern the sort of response that Cone had hoped to generate: critical reflection upon the shortcomings of white theology. As early as 1970, Herzog claimed that salvation has become liberation, not only liberation from oppression, but liberation of white people from false constructions of the human being: "Resisting white man's self-delusions is liberation from sin and error. Resisting man's inhumanity to man is—God's liberation."[51] From the outset, Herzog understood the linkage between racial injustice in America and the economic prosperity that has been borne on the backs of people of color. He thus tied the liberation of white Americans to their liberation from "wealth for wealth's sake" and the subsequent "exploitation of the neighbor."[52] Fully human existence is posited as lacking in both oppressor and oppressed, and Herzog recognizes a particular vocation to address the white American's dehumanization of self and others.

Herzog's *Liberation Theology: Liberation in Light of the Fourth Gospel* brought this theme out more pointedly and in greater depth. Here Herzog proposes that theology must begin to "think black," by which he means:

(1) We have to learn to "think black" theologically. To "think white" is to turn in upon the Cartesian self, to engage in "navel-gazing." . . . To "think black" means to be able to think from the perspective of the underdog. . . . (2) To think from the perspective of the oppressed, however, is not yet to think theologically. "Thinking black" . . . has to be radically tied to the originating event of the Christian faith. In fact, ultimately we can "think black" only if we are bound to the originating event.[53]

Herzog then concludes with this christological imperative: "To speak of this theology as liberation theology is to imply that the identification of Jesus Christ with the wretched of the earth not merely brought freedom of the individual, but also gave him public space for freedom to become operative."[54] In this way, Herzog calls for a "radical *metanoia*" among white theologians, which moves away from liberal theology's emphasis on the "bourgeois self" of white Americans who, unlike the oppressed of the earth, have "the time and the freedom to reflect on their precious, private selves."[55] It points toward a communal, social, structural reality and not merely individual and privatized existence. Herzog's liberation theology is Christ-centered, biblically grounded, and ethically responsible. Theologically, the true human being, whether black or white, can emerge only when a theological method of liberation replaces individualistic, self-reflective white liberal theology.

In 1974, Herzog's challenge to white theology began, perhaps, to show a level of frustration as he posed the question, "Will the liberation of white theology ever be possible?"[56] Already in 1974, lamented Herzog, the cry for justice of the 1960s had been muted. The heart of the matter for Herzog was the white theologian who feared change. Overcoming such fear requires recognizing the economic disparities that have driven much of modern theology: "A first step might be the realization that over the centuries, Protestant theology has largely stood aside from peoples outcast, downtrodden, humiliated. It has served the rich, the successful, the property owners. So people who could not afford an enterprise called theology see it as "white theology" standing against them."[57] At this juncture, Herzog continues to take the racialized nature of white theology to heart, but he begins to consider economics and the poor as the crux of liberation theology. Indeed, in his 1988 work, *God-Walk*, Herzog used the term that, a decade later, would become the focus of a good deal of theology, "empire." He writes, "One of the major metaphors we can no longer escape is empire. . . . Accountable teaching—growing out of God-walk and focused in liberation theology—means resisting empire as idol: resisting what today competes most with God."[58] Echoes of Constantinian Christianity appear as the focal point for Herzog's work.

In excavating Herzog's theological anthropology, it is clear that he understood human liberation in terms of both the oppressed and oppressor, as indicated above. Furthermore, he defines authentic humanity in terms of the liberated consciousness, which enables a person to become "black" in the sense of releasing "one's identity as the superior white self."[59] In Herzog's reading, new life in Christ releases the white person from bondage to a false image of the self. The individualistic self constructed by the white majority is a false representation and is exposed as such in the encounter with the *homo liber*, the free man, the true self, the image of God, Jesus.[60] In this liberating encounter, the individual enters into a "corporate selfhood."[61] In this encounter with the liberating Jesus, "we find the black (and the red) as neighbor, and vice versa. [Humanity] is not [humanity] without the black (and the red)."[62] As such, resurrected life points toward life together as one human race, toward the willingness "to live together with [one's] definite neighbor forever. . . . Only in being willing to live with the black and to face him forever will the [white person] understand the resurrection."[63] Being human, then, is conceived of as a corporate structure in which all persons can experience the fullness of life. Moreover, for Herzog, "what makes [us] truly human is freedom," defined in terms of the mutual "sharing in transcendent freedom."[64] Yet fully human existence remains a future possibility, as the *imago Dei* is not yet realized. To become fully human is a process that begins with becoming one with the oppressed.

As Herzog concludes his interpretation of John, he describes the existing milieu as a situation in which there is an increasing concentration of economic and military wealth in the hands of the white majority in the United States, which is actually a white *minority* in terms of the world's population. In subsequent writings, Herzog will emphasize this concern for economic justice. Indeed, it is appropriate to note that he was utterly prophetic in his articulation of the economic trajectory toward the concentration of more and more wealth in the hands of fewer and fewer. While racism recedes into the background in his later writings, the concern for fully human existence remains evident. Not only does he introduce *God-Walk* by mentioning the ways that "unreasonable theological rationality" has prevented theologians from hearing black theology, but he continues his claim made first in *Liberation Theology* which equates being born again with becoming black.[65]

Herzog appropriated the critique and questions raised by black theology, listened to the voices of the numerous strands of liberation theology that emerged, and constructed a white theology of liberation. Herzog's theology certainly had a level of influence on later generations of scholars, yet the engagement of Herzog's theology by white theologians has been circumscribed. Perhaps, in part, Herzog's movement away from the critical question of race and racial injustice and into a more global perspective limited his ability to speak with authority to the North American context. This in no way suggests that economics and class issues are unimportant, nor does it seek to dismiss the synergy of race, class, gender, and other systems of oppression within the context of the United States. However, the power of racist discourse and practice, as well as the systemic oppression of minoritized racial and ethnic persons in America, continues to reflect America's "original sin" and begs the question of whether white theologians are willing to make the naming and dismantling of white supremacy central to their theological discourse.

Why did the question of race seemingly grow to be less central in Herzog's work? No doubt his critique of white theology led to criticism and ostracism by many in his scholarly community, under the rubric of liberation theology's "marginal" value. No doubt the evidence of economic injustice was also growing. Nonetheless, though the civil rights era reshaped the legal contours of the nation, racist discourse and practice remains despite and because of racism's more subtle and elusive nature. The lived experience of people of color indicates they still cannot step outside the question of race as a defining reality within the United States, unlike their white counterparts who can slip into the comfortable and invisible cloak of whiteness.

Peter Hodgson also addressed the racist discourse and practice of American society and theology. In 1974, he published *Children of Freedom: Black Liberation in Christian Perspective* and quickly followed in 1976, with *New Birth of Freedom: A Theology of Bondage and Liberation*. In studying the peculiar nature of bondage and freedom in America, Hodgson considers the history of oppression within this nation. It is a philosophical approach that seeks to analyze phenomenologically the structures of human freedom. As with Herzog's early liberation theology, Hodgson's *New Birth of Freedom* responds to and incorporates black theology and the challenge of James Cone, though Hodgson also makes clear his reluctance to identify with any one liberation movement and his deliberate engagement with the literature of various theologies of liberation.[66] Significantly, he recognizes that his "situation as a white American male, is one shaped by forefathers who sought to bring forth on this continent 'a new nation, conceived in liberty,' and who enslaved blacks, dispossessed Indians, and subjugated women in the process."[67] It is this primary paradox of the nation's ideals and the realities of oppression that he seeks to interpret and reconstruct. Hodgson thus begins his argument by highlighting the historical exploitation of Native Americans, African Americans, and women.

Yet, following this historical analysis, something peculiar occurs as he develops the meaning of freedom in relation to being human. The voices and historical experiences with which he opens are largely, though not entirely, left behind. On the one hand, Herzog is concerned to construct a liberating theology which can resolve the paradoxical, discriminatory nature of American society. But on the other hand, Herzog seemingly maintains an intellectual regard for the normativity of white male theologians. Certainly, there were few publications by scholars of color in the seventies; at least, few recent theologies upon which to draw, and he does reference Cone, Juan Luis Segundo, Major Jones, and others briefly. Clearly, Hodgson does not dismiss theologians of color, as he attends in some detail to the important black theological debate around the question of theodicy.[68] Nevertheless, it is hard to shake the suspicion that the white theological tradition remains normative for him, even as he wishes to further the cause of fully human existence.

Hodgson's 1989 *God in History*, which undertakes a Hegelian account of or framework for freedom, continues to raise questions about the normativity of whiteness. In response to the rise of postmodernism and the problematic relationship between God and salvation history that resulted from this Western intellectual paradigm shift, he reinterprets Hegel's meta-historical vision: "Instead of speaking of a single, more or less unified and progressive history of freedom, I believe today we must speak of a plurality of partial, fragmentary, always ambiguous histories of freedom, struggling to survive, and sometimes prevailing, against the forces of domination and oppression."[69] Thus, Hodgson acknowledges and continues to investigate the nature of oppression. Nevertheless, few theologians or philosophers of color are resources for his constructive argument. Cone, William R. Jones, and Gustavo Gutiérrez receive nods, but many more white feminist theologians are woven into his argument, as well as plethora of white North American and European male theologians and philosophers. Perhaps Hodgson's strategy is to develop a compelling argument for freedom and liberation for the oppressed based upon the majority culture's own canon. Yet, even if that is the case, it cannot help but appear paternalistic and oddly unresponsive to and dialogically bereft of the voices of those he purports to accompany toward freedom. The suspicion that Hodgson holds an epistemological preference for the white Western theological tradition remains credible.

This suspicion seems to be reinforced in his 1994 textbook, *Winds of the Spirit: A Constructive Christian Theology*.[70] In Part 2, "Contextualizing," Hodgson introduces the problem of postmodernity before addressing ongoing oppression and the search for freedom. The challenge of late modernity, he argues, is the question of God's absence. This state of crisis leads to the historical moment when transformation is possible, beginning with widespread transformations of consciousness.[71] He then proceeds to introduce briefly various liberation theologies (Latin American, Asian, "African American," and Feminist). But when one turns to his chapter, "Human Being: Finite Freedom, Fall, Sin, and Evil," theologians of color are conspicuously absent. His anthropological argument arises out of his vision in *New Birth of Freedom*, but revised to incorporate the theology of Edward Farley instead of Paul Ricoeur. In addition to Farley, Herzog relies on Hegel, Husserl, Heidegger, Jaspers, Levinas, Rahner, Tillich, Pannenberg, and others.[72] If his primary interests are in freedom as characteristic of human being and in theology that "is grounded in experience," then his reliance on the white Western intellectual tradition belies his intention.[73] One must respond with the question: Whose freedom and experience?

While Hodgson does note that "African American theology reminds us that racism is one of the most destructive and illusory forms of human idolatry," he names no theologians who have done that reminding either in the text or a footnote. Hodgson also devotes a section to the dominion of "worldly powers," with attention to racism, sexism, naturism, homophobia, and xenophobia. But the section on racism remains silent on sources, other than a footnote that points to George Kelsey's 1965 work and his own conversation with black theology, *Children of Freedom*. Symbolically, by referring readers to the bibliography of his own book, he subsumes and inscribes the theologians of color within his white majority culture perspective. While such a move is likely unintentional, it nonetheless marginalizes the very voices he claims to support and uphold. Thus, Hodgson's commitment to dismantling racist structures is disemboweled, as he settles back into his whiteness and dialogue with white, primarily male, interlocutors. The trajectory of Hodgson's theological anthropology moves increasingly away from engaging and exposing the reality of racism. While naming human experience as central to the theological task, his texts privilege the white experience in America. Can a theological anthropology that intends to be liberatory achieve its stated objective if those whose direct experience of oppression are left silent, relegated to an occasional footnote, and virtually invisible?

Given the significance of basic Christian theology textbooks in shaping theological and ecclesial understanding, we must also examine if and how those authored or edited by white theologians attend to racialized discourse and practice. In this case, to Hodgson's credit, his introductory text actually does better than most at naming racialized discourse and practice as a point of engagement for envisioning fully human existence. Other theological textbooks authored by white men and women receive mixed reviews in terms of giving careful attention to questions of race and racism.

Daniel Migliore's *Faith Seeking Understanding* approaches theological anthropology with the basic claim that "to be human is to live freely and gladly in relationships of mutual respect and love."[74] The image of God suggests that fully human existence is located in relationship to God or a prior action by the divine, but theological anthropology "cannot ignore the findings of cultural anthropology, psychology, sociology, and other disciplines" in considering the meaning of human being.[75] In other words, a nuanced and deep account of fully human existence requires attention to the diverse and complex ways human beings experience life. Migliore mentions race, class, and gender, noting that context may shift the meaning of "sin" for a particular group of people. He names racism as an example of the distorted interpretation of "dominion" and notes that sin as "self-exaltation" and as "self-abnegation" cuts across race, class, and gender.[76] These points indicate that he recognizes the importance of racialized discourse and practice. Nevertheless, throughout his theological anthropology, he is far more engaged with the white Western tradition and white feminist theologians than scholars of color. Jacquelyn Grant is the only theologian of color named, and that single reference is found only in one footnote.

Not Every Spirit (1995) by Christopher Morse provides an example of white theological anthropologies devoid of any consideration of racism. His chapter on humanity is framed by a quote from Karl Barth, suggesting that "a great deal about us can be explained by the fact that we are continually hungry, sexually unsettled, and in need of sleep."[77] Framing his chapter on theological anthropology in this way will enable Morse to focus on issues of gender and sexuality in relation to fully human existence. Morse proceeds to the objection that many doctrines of humanity order human existence "to the exclusion of humanity's actual diversity."[78] Dismantling normative arguments of male and female roles and stereotypical thinking stemming from interpretations of Genesis, he then considers the dualism of "higher and lower natures" as it manifests in the notion of male superiority.[79] Although both of these problematic claims could address race and racism, Morse remains silent on the topic throughout the chapter, with the exception of one passing comment about "ethnic or genetic privilege."[80]

While one could blame Morse's reticence on his indebtedness to Barth and the quote from Barth that frames his account, Joerg Rieger has demonstrated that Barth actually wrestled with racism. Rieger quotes Barth's *Ethics*, the very same publication from which Morse extracted the framing quote, but with an entirely different perspective:

> When members of the white race all enjoy every possible intellectual and material advantage on the basis of the superiority of one race and the sub-jection of many other races, and of the use that for centuries our race has made of both, I myself may not have harmed a single hair on the heads of Africans or Indians. . . . Yet I am still a member of the white race. . . . My share in the sin against Asia or Africa for the last hundred or fifty years may be very remote or indirect, but would Europe be what it is, and would I be what I am, if that expansion had never happened?[81]

Barth's understanding of racist discourse and practice expressed within this single quote in Rieger's work speaks volumes in comparison to Morse's silence on race. Morse, who is on the faculty at Union Seminary in New York City surely could not claim unawareness of such issues, yet he chooses not to engage white privilege or questions of race in his exposition of theological anthropology.

Although *Christian Theology: An Introduction*, now in its fifth edition, is written by British theologian Alister McGrath, it bears inclusion here if only for its ongoing use within theological schools in the United States.[82] Writing from an evangelical and Anglican perspective, McGrath attempts to bring both historical and contemporary (primarily from the midtwentieth century) trajectories together as he introduces the basic loci of the Christian faith. Yet his chapter on theological anthropology is bereft of any sense of contextualization other than a section on Weberian analysis of capitalism. McGrath's *Christian Theology* provides the white reader with a sense of neutrality and apparent universalism as the normativity of whiteness guides the theological anthropology and each doctrine. Ultimately, many white Americans consider a text such as McGrath's as balanced and attentive to the tradition, but does the theological vision articulated therein prepare persons for encountering human beings in the twenty-first century and facilitating the fully human existence of all persons, not only those of the majority white culture?

Finally, the Jones and Lakeland edited volume, *Constructive Theology*, is a promising alternative, as the editors bring together various voices and perspectives within each chapter.[83] Chapter 2, "Human Being," begins with a racialized example from the Montgomery bus boycott along with vignettes related to sexuality and gender. The authors of the chapter address freedom and responsibility, identity and alterity, and time and memory as central to understanding human being. These issues bring traditional theological considerations into the context of the contemporary society. Not unlike Morse's treatment, issues related to gender and sexism are addressed throughout the chapter, though specific engagement with race and racism is left to be examined in Shawn Copeland's concluding essay. On the one hand, this approach provides for a deeper assessment of the ways in which race and racism are implicated in considerations of fully human existence. Yet, on the other, it leaves the African American voice to raise these questions, such that the white theologians need not wrestle deeply with their own white privilege. Moreover, it projects an "additive" method in which the white theological tradition might appear to be normative and supplemented by theologians of color. No doubt, this was not the intention of the authors. But the printed text, in fact, may belie their goal of presenting diverse perspectives as authoritative alongside more traditional ones.

This brief survey of introductory textbooks is not intended to be exhaustive but illustrative of the ways white privilege continues to take center stage. Given that white supremacy systematically silenced voices of color for generations, these texts will necessarily include white male theological contributions throughout history. All of these textbooks have great strengths and offer in-depth attention to the development and construction of Christian doctrine. Yet, when we read theologians of color, the centrality of race and racism to theological anthropology remains a priority. To conceptualize the meaning of human being without recognizing one's ongoing dehumanization would lack truthfulness and lead to meaninglessness, even reinforcing the dehumanizing forces. As a result, we would anticipate that introductory textbooks would at least acknowledge the ways that Scripture and theology have been used to dehumanize persons of color. When theological anthropologies emphasize gender equality, they rightly expose the systemic sin of sexism. However, in doing so, they may unconsciously or quite intentionally reinforce the normativity of whiteness.

There is much work yet to be done in both scrutinizing the writings of white theologians of the past and in critiquing the theologies of contemporary writers, as a means to further the conscientization process. Perhaps one of the key elements in this conscientization of white Americans is the rewriting and rereading of history from the perspective of those who have been marginalized, dehumanized, assimilated, and annihilated by Christian faith and theology in the service of economics, politics, and power. To unravel white privilege and white supremacy in theology and the church begins with the activities of demystifying and demythologizing the history of racism, to which we turn in chapter 3.

3

ASHES TO ASHES

The past is a bucket of ashes.

—*Carl Sandburg*

The rearview mirror reflected a white man in his forties. "How long have you been in this country?" he asked. "All my life," I replied, wincing. . . . He replied, "I was wondering because your English is excellent!" Then I explained, "My grandfather came here from Japan in the 1880s. My family has been here, in America, for over a hundred years." He glanced at me in the mirror. To him, I did not look American. . . . He saw me through a filter—what I call the Master Narrative of American History. According to this powerful and popular but inaccurate story, our country was settled by European immigrants, and Americans are "white." Not to be "white" is to be designated as the "Other"—different, inferior, and unassimilable.

—*Ronald Takaki*

You may write me down in history . . .
But still, like dust, I'll rise.

—*Maya Angelou*

The season of Lent opens with the reminder, "From dust you have come and to dust you shall return." We Christians believe in salvation history. God has been at work since the dawn of creation in the drama of fully human existence with its delicate combination of free will and freedom, finitude and potential, brokenness and redemption. We believe that Christ has died, Christ is risen, Christ will come again. Salvation history is not simply future-oriented, but is rooted and grounded in the past acts of God in Jesus Christ and the present activity of God in the Holy Spirit. God in Christ will come again to complete the new creation, a creation of love and the fullness of love. Yet, despite the salvation history proclaimed by Christians, Christianity in the United States, shaped in the image of white Americans, has written a starkly different story that has undermined God's creation and the hope of countless human beings.

The poet Carl Sandburg began his "Four Preludes on Playthings of the Wind," with the inscription, "The past is a bucket of ashes." Often we think of the past as little more than ashes through which we might sift to discover fragmentary remains of our ancestors. No longer living beings, the ashes might contain some intriguing relics but lack the vitality to influence or shape the present. Yet anyone who has left ashes in a flammable container knows that a bucket of ashes contains smoldering embers that retain the potential to ignite and do great harm. Those ashes are not yet dead to us. The past lives on in multifarious ways, structuring and forming our lives and relationships and, in especially significant ways, the freedom, opportunity, and fully human existence of minoritized racial and ethnic communities. To ignore the past, as the philosopher George Santayana reminds us, is to be condemned to repeat it. Better yet, we might rephrase Santayana to suggest that to ignore the past reflects, perhaps, an intention to repeat it, if doing so is construed as somehow advantageous.

In the ongoing "Master Narrative of American History," to use the phrase of historian Ronald Takaki in referring to the end of the metanarrative, history is inscribed within the normativity of whiteness. We may have a month, week, or day in which "we" *include* (an action conveying the intent to draw into the center of whiteness) other racial and ethnic groups, but their story is always posited as secondary, inferior, less central to the nation's "real" history. Unless we recognize the influence of white privilege and white supremacy in shaping the long and painful national narrative, racism will continue to reinvent and reinscribe itself as the defining reality in the United States, even as white Americans inch ever closer to becoming a numerical minority. Racism and racist discourse and practice have been so integral to the history and development of the United States and so tied to Christianity that, at times, they function to reorder our consciousness to assume such racist structures are normal and neutral, even scriptural. Our epistemological lenses are framed by the norm of whiteness and its triumphant progress across history. In reality, racist structures and systems may be dubbed and proclaimed as normative, but theologically, they are neither normative—in the sense that white supremacy is inconsistent with the gospel of Jesus Christ—nor neutral. To the contrary, racist discourse and practice seeks to reinforce the political, economic, and ecclesial power of whiteness at the expense of minoritized racial and ethnic communities. In this case, to be "neutral" is to reinforce and replicate the very American version of Constantinian Christianity.

As a result of this epistemological prerogative, it is not sufficient to relate simply a brief version of American religious history, even one that includes diverse voices, since the intersection of Christianity with economics, politics, and power has a synergistic or compounding effect on the problem of racism. Only a broader view can provide the depth of perspective and comprehension to break open the racist logic of American history and its repetitive or recurring nature. Even today, most histories are told from the perspective of the white majority culture in a narrative of the triumph of Manifest Destiny, of God's chosen people as they conquer the New World and create the noblest of all societies. But when we gather the stories from the underside, from the margins, and from those perspectives long silenced by the powerful majority, a different portrait begins to emerge, one that reminds us that the United States, like any other human institution, is flawed and in need of the transforming power of grace. The terms "underside" and "margins" themselves indicate the normative nature of whiteness, the power of the majority culture to name that which is center. We are also reminded that, although the center of whiteness has attempted to exclude others from the central narrative and suppress their stories, minoritized racial and ethnic communities have played a pivotal role in resisting dehumanization and providing the stimulus to reform systems toward more just and truthful representations of American and Christian ideals.

Some historians have sought to rectify the partiality of the Master Narrative by examining the perspectives and story lines most often neglected, disregarded as insignificant, or incorporated partially and selectively from the white perspective. One recent example is Christian historian Mark Noll's *God and Race in American Politics*, which provides a brief but illuminating survey of the interrelationship of religion, race, and politics in the United States. Noll captures the essence of why historical understanding is so crucial to unraveling the logic of white privilege: "Race and religion have acted together powerfully not only to shape the nation's political history, but also to define the nation's central moral problem."[1] Consequently, instead of promoting a more just society, Christianity is often implicated in the moral lapses of the nation's racist discourse and practice. Although

Noll acknowledges the impact of American religious dynamics upon all minoritized racial and ethnic groups, he focuses his investigation on the black/white relationship, since the American racial problem is most visible in this binary dynamic.

In a second monograph, *The Arrogance of Faith*, which also emphasizes the black/white dilemma with some attention to First Peoples, Forrest G. Wood argues that "Christianity, in the five centuries since its message was first carried to the peoples of the New World—and, in particular, to the natives and the transplanted Africans of English North America and the United States—has been fundamentally racist in its ideology, organization, and practice."[2] Although providing insights into racially motivated Christian discourse and practice from the nation's founding up to the twentieth century, Wood biases his argument by focusing on the ways Christianity has reinforced white supremacy, while neglecting the countervailing narratives arising from the margins or underside of history. In other words, his critique of Constantinian Christianity neglects the powerful expressions of Prophetic Christianity that have challenged the evolving racist discourse and practice since the nation's inception. In his eagerness to discredit white Christendom, he also neglects and marginalizes, to an extent, those communities with whom he intends to stand in solidarity.

Particularly helpful is Ronald Takaki's *A Different Mirror*. Although not focused specifically on the history of Christianity in relation to race in America, it weaves together the histories of minoritized racial and ethnic groups since the founding of colonies on the eastern shores of North America through the end of the twentieth century. This narrative of American history provides an epistemological reorientation by attending to the nation's development from the perspective of minoritized racial and ethic communities and their contributions to a society that has alternately viewed them in terms of utility and disposability. The significance of Takaki's approach to a comprehensive historical inquiry refusing to accord white Americans the privileged position is twofold. First, it demonstrates clearly the systematic nature of the racist logic at work in the United States across time and place. Second, it pushes back against the isolation and marginalization of individual groups that tend to create a binary structure of investigation and minimize the racism that has been perpetuated against all groups considered to be "other-than-white." One racialized narrative told in light of white supremacy inadequately expresses the correlative and compounding reality of the experiences of distinct minoritized racial and ethnic groups. The nation was built not only by means of red land and black labor but also brown land, brown labor, and yellow labor. Groups such as the Irish and Italians competed and conspired to become "white" once they arrived on the shores of North America and became aware of the benefits accruing to whiteness. The history of the nation has been painted in neutral tones, as predominantly white, but the richer, more complex palette of colors reveals our inhumanity under the guise of Christian love. The first step toward systemic change and renewed relationship is always the awakening of the conscience to morally deficient ways of relating to others and to God.

In attempting to trace, however inadequately, the history of racism in the United States, we will adopt the strategy that Cornel West describes as "demythologizing" and "demystifying." These complementary processes are defined in relationship to the meaning of socially constructed practices such as racism: "Demythologization is a *mapping* activity that reconstructs and redescribes forms of signification for the purpose of situating them in the dynamic flow of social practices. Demystification is a *theoretical* activity that attempts to give explanations that account for the role and function of specific social practices."[3]

The demythologizing or mapping activity that follows seeks to include and illuminate the racism toward African Americans, Native Americans, Latino/as, and Asian Americans. Too often these histories are separated and examined in isolation, but from the earliest European footsteps and encampments in North America, the histories of these "races" have intersected and confronted one another. When considered together, these racialized histories offer insight into the function of racism in building a white democracy and capitalist society that self-identifies as Christian. Even so, the intention is neither to conflate these quite distinct histories and thereby ignore the different experiences and perspectives nor to offer stereotypical renderings of any group of minoritized racial and ethnic persons. Neither do we wish somehow to impose a privileged white perspective on these histories as a normative accounting, though this danger is ever present. Instead, the intention is to avoid separate histories of marginalized groups that dilute the heights, depths, and breadth of American racism. A more reliable demythologizing process seeks to combine these narratives and to discern patterns among and between them.

In terms of the demystification process, our focus in this chapter will remain on the theological question of human being and fully human existence as it relates to three broad periods in the racist and racialized history of the United States: (1) Pre–Civil War racism, a period in which whiteness questions whether minoritized racial and ethnic groups are human or a different species, as white privilege and power are consolidated; (2) racism from the Civil War through the civil rights movement of the 1960s, characterized by the scientific quest to maintain white dominance by asserting the inferior or subhuman nature of minoritized racial and ethnic groups; and (3) the contemporary discourse on racism, which presumes racist discourse and practice is an individual phenomenon at worst and nonexistent at best. Contemporary racism, which sociologists refer to as "modern racism" or "color-blind racism," reconstructs racist discourses under the cloak of neutrality, while perpetuating social practices that discriminate against and diminish the life and possibilities of persons of color. In every period, minoritized racial and ethnic peoples resisted and rejected the racist discourse and practice and its dehumanizing telos.

This periodization serves to facilitate our understanding of a complex racial narrative, but is far from being comprehensive or definitive. It is intellectually and epistemologically impossible to narrate a complete accounting of these histories, but we can provide one that consciously attends to minoritized racial and ethnic communities and their experiences. Even so, we are reminded that over thirty years ago, Vine Deloria Jr. asserted that the focus on history and historical narratives is a function of the myopic Western (i.e., white European) world view, in contrast to the Native American perspective in which spatial realities are the organizing principle.[4] Thus, the periodization that follows remains embedded in a Eurocentric epistemological trajectory even as it attempts to attend to the multiplicity of experiences and thereby decenter whiteness.

From the Pilgrims' Arrival to the Civil War

Since the days prior to its inception when "pilgrims," "colonists," or even, "colonizers" first set foot in the "New World" (ironically, seeking the religious freedom they would soon deny to others), the United States has struggled with racist discourse and practice manifested in various forms and embedded in institutions and systems, including Christian ones. Before the arrival of European and English colonists, Native Americans expressed their full humanity and cultural identity on the North American continent. As Homer Noley suggests, when

Native Americans first encountered white people, they saw only other "people" not another "race."[5] Of course, humans were not the only people that existed, as all created things were considered people without hierarchical or qualitative ordering. The First Peoples knew no Great Chain of Being, only the Great Spirit who created all forms of people. By contrast, early white settlers viewed the indigenous people as uncivilized, unchristian "savages" and, under the logic of the Doctrine of Discovery, they began claiming ownership of the land that had been inhabited and cultivated by the Native tribes for thousands of years.[6]

Simultaneously, though they had once been free to express their full humanity and cultural identity across the African continent, Africans were taken from their homelands by way of the West Indies on ships of death, bought and sold on American soil, and forced to develop the nation's agricultural economy on their backs while owners paternalistically claimed that enslavement would make them human, civilized, Christian. The fundamental requirements of the fledgling United States economy—what has sometimes been called red land and black labor—were entangled from the outset with racist discourse and practice, though particular forms of theological justification would ebb and flow from era to era. While the Southern states were directly implicated in the practice of slavery long after the North had prohibited it, the Northern states were likewise implicated in the quest for land and cheap labor, and both North and South constructed racial discourses of superiority/inferiority, subhuman, or less-than-human as justification for these immoral acts.

The earliest racial discourses functioned to create legal definitions of what it means to be human and not-quite-human, thus justifying the loss and limiting of freedom and self-determination, as well as life itself, for certain categories or types of people. Prior to the arrival of the Europeans, Native Americans in the area of today's United States numbered somewhere around five million.[7] Whatever their language, they usually referred to themselves as "the people" or "people."[8] Rather than identifying themselves as some "ethnic" or "racial" group, they simply understood themselves as one kind of people who populate the earth. Animals, trees, flowers, rivers, even rocks were people in this holistic and relational world view. But the narratives of the white settlers soon began to dehumanize and destroy the First Peoples. Despite the fact that Native Americans often helped the colonists survive their initial days and years in North America by sharing food and agricultural knowledge, the attempt to annihilate or assimilate began early. By 1623, the

English colonists in Jamestown, for example, launched the so-called "first Indian war," which was intended to be a "deliberate and systematic destruction of the Powhatan Confederacy."[9] Such wars would continue for the next three hundred years, systematically destroying tribe after tribe. Of course, the immigrants not only wrought physical violence upon the Natives but also brought diseases, forced migration, and sought to eliminate Native cultural traditions, including matriarchal societies, in favor of the Christian "way of life." Early colonists understood their mission as one of propagating the gospel and Christianizing the "heathens." Thomas Gossett points out that, "the Englishmen frequently professed that conversion of the Indians and Negroes was one of their chief aims. [But] they did not succeed so well as did the Spanish in converting the Indians or in assimilating Indians and Negroes into their own society."[10] When assimilation fails, elimination becomes the alternative.

Although, initially, European goods were exchanged by colonists for land and assistance from the Natives, soon the Europeans desired to acquire more land. At the end of the Seven Years' War in 1763, the English king "issued a proclamation designed to sharply limit the taking of additional Indian land by the colonists. The colonists, however, largely ignored it, frequently invading Indian territory and stealing land."[11] After the Revolutionary War, the new US government officially considered tribes as sovereign foreign nations and sought to maintain good relations with them. Laws were passed in 1787, 1790, and 1793 aimed at protecting tribal lands from encroachment. Of course, such mandates were difficult to enforce and westward expansion repeatedly violated these federal laws, pushing the tribes farther west. Within fifty years, under the presidency of Andrew Jackson, the federal government's attitude shifted toward the blatant appropriation of tribal lands and disregard of Native rights. In 1830, Congress passed the Indian Removal Act, which relocated tribes from the southern and southeastern United States to areas west of the Mississippi. Many Eastern tribes, of course, had already been displaced during colonial days. Although tribes resisted, they were forced, often brutally, to relocate to the Oklahoma and Indian Territories. The so-called "Five Civilized Tribes" (i.e., the Chickasaw, Cherokee, Choctaw, Creek, and Seminole tribes) were part of this forced relocation, and the "Trail of Tears" of the Cherokee people is especially well documented, though the other tribes had similar forced marches under inhuman conditions, having been deprived of their land and personal property.[12] Russell Thornton notes that the designation by white society of "civilized" indicated that these tribes "had accepted some non-Indian, that is European or American, lifeways."[13] "Civilized" or not, Christian or not, they were denied the right to live on their tribal lands which the white Americans wished to possess, arguing that the Native peoples were not "using" or cultivating and developing the land. Adopting white cultural norms and the Christian faith proved insufficient for the First Peoples to enter into the privileges of whiteness.

The "civilizing" process imposed upon the Native Americans included attempts to convert them to Christianity and to educate them in the white ways. The Puritans, who had survived their first years in America through the aid of Native Americans, soon began to impose laws to control them. Native peoples were prohibited from undertaking any activity on the Christian Sabbath, and "death was the penalty for blasphemy, which was said to include refusal to accept 'the colonist's religion.' "[14] Educating children into European ways was also a priority: "By 1887, more than two hundred schools had been established under federal supervision, with an enrollment of over fourteen thousand Indian children, many of whom were forcibly removed from their families."[15] The infamous quote from Richard H. Pratt attests to the brutality of this Christianizing process: "Kill the Indian in him, and save the man." Throughout this era and into the next, children were punished for using their Native languages and were not allowed to wear traditional clothing or to practice their religious rites. Whether Native peoples attempted to assimilate into white culture by force or by choice, it made little difference in the ways they were viewed and treated. White immigrants, self-proclaimed "good Christians," were greedy for land and wealth and created narratives of subhuman peoples unable to conform to civilized norms. Hence, God intended the white man to govern and occupy the land. By 1800, the population of Native peoples in the United States had dwindled to 600,000 and by the end of the nineteenth century their numbers are estimated at a mere 250,000.[16] Not only had they been stripped of their freedom to live and work on lands they had occupied for centuries, but genocide of massive proportions had occurred.

As the systematic destruction and dehumanization of the Native peoples began, the slave trade was well underway, leading to a second genocide. In 1526, the first African slaves arrived in South Carolina. During the sixteenth century, Spanish explorers and merchants had enslaved Native Americans, perhaps as many as tens of thousands of Native people. But in 1542, Spain outlawed this practice, which fueled the African slave trade.[17] By the end of the seventeenth century, Slave Codes emerged. Although they varied by state, "the general point of view expressed in most of them was the same: slaves are not people but property; laws should protect the ownership of such property and should also protect whites against any dangers that might arise."[18] Slave Codes also ensured that slaves would remain in a subordinate status to the white population. By 1860 there were almost four million enslaved Africans and their descendants, primarily working within the agricultural economy of the Southern colonies and states.[19] Cotton transformed the American economy, and chattel slavery was the engine that drove this expansion.[20]

The Constitutional Convention of 1787, which provided for representation of slaves, was a defining moment. In the debate over representation in Congress, Southern states wanted slaves to be counted; Northern states argued that, as property, slaves should not be represented in Congress. The compromise written into the Constitution (Article I, section 2) counted slaves as three-fifths of a person. The irony here is unmistakable. The Northern states, the bastion of antislavery sentiments, fought against considering slaves as fully human. No doubt, it was a move aimed at political control and could be justified under the guise of controlling Congress and, thus, enabling it to move the country toward abolishing chattel slavery. Nevertheless, the Constitution, which would establish the freedoms of Americans, inscribed enslaved black people as less than fully human. While the Northern states abolished slavery—at least in part because the Northern economy was less dependent on agriculture—black Americans were still not free citizens. The North may have decried slavery, but it did not dismiss racism. Indeed, Franklin and Moss point out that, although "free" blacks did have substantial legal status during the Revolutionary period, "after that time . . . their status deteriorated, until toward the end of the slave period the distinction between slaves and free blacks had diminished to a point where in some instances it was hardly discernable."[21]

To be sure, slaves resisted their dehumanization and subjugation. Slave rebellions and escapes were common, and religion emerged as a primary form of resistance. The Black Church tradition originated in slave religion, then adopted Protestant Christianity, despite slave masters who "feared that enslaved Blacks who embraced Christianity would interpret their new religious status as a step toward freedom, justice, and equality."[22] Indeed, the Christian religion would provide African Americans with a narrative of liberation—a subversive prophetic discourse—as well as an organization or a location where they could exercise self-determination apart from white society. As the authors of *Black Church Studies* claim, after the Revolutionary War, "independent Black churches quickly became the core of African American communities in their quest for freedom from domination from white ecclesiastical bodies and other expressions of white supremacy."[23] While white Americans tried to force Native Americans to accept Christian religion and assimilate into white culture, African Americans embraced Christian faith (possibly because aspects of Christianity resonated with African tribal religions) and used it as a means to claim their freedom, self-determination, and full humanity. Nonetheless, during this era Native and African Americans alike resisted domination by white society, even as their freedom and humanity were limited by legal, political, social, and religious discourses and practices.

This era also bears witness to the rise of racial classifications, beginning with a French physician by the name of François Bernier in the late seventeenth century, who described four classifications of human beings: Europeans, Far Easterners, Negroes, and Lapps. "The significance of Bernier's observations," notes Gossett, "lies in the fact that his is probably the first attempt in history to classify all the races."[24] Such attempts at categorization would dominate racial theory for the next three hundred years. In the eighteenth century, as anthropology developed, scientists differentiated "species" from "varieties" within the species, which occurred primarily as a result of variations in geography and climate. Thus, in the taxonomy of the Swedish naturalist Carl Linnaeus, the one human species has four discernable varieties, which differ from those described by Bernier: *Homo Europaeus, Homo Asiaticus, Homo Afer,* and *Homo Americanus.*[25] For Johann Blumenbach, five races were discernable: Caucasian, Mongolian, Ethiopian, American, and Malay.[26] From system to system, the groupings differed according to the perspective of the architect, thereby suggesting the arbitrary nature of racial classifications. Although most eighteenth century attempts at classification posited the equality of the races as varieties within the human species, some such as the French naturalist George Buffon, begin to argue for the normativity and superiority of the white race.[27]

These eighteenth century European theories and classifications of the races were known to educated persons in the United States where many Americans accepted the essential unity of the human species.

Presbyterian minister and professor, Samuel Stanhope Smith, argued in favor of the essential equality of the races. He contended that no accurate system of classification was possible due to the climatic and geographical factors, as well as discriminatory practices which caused variation. Hence, altered circumstances and environments would produce more white-like features: If persons of African descent, "were perfectly free, enjoyed property, and were admitted to a liberal participation of the society, rank and privileges of their masters, they would change their African peculiarities much faster."[28] Smith's theory does not reflect an entirely liberated perspective; after all, he also argued that field slaves looked more "African" than did the house slaves who were more civilized (and, by inference, more white-like). Gossett suggests that there remained a pervasive sense of the innate potential of all races as "both science and theology were in agreement except for a few dissenters."[29]

Even so, the prominence of some of those dissenters should not be minimized. Thomas Jefferson, in his *Notes on Virginia* (1786) argued for the inferiority of black persons and even questioned whether they might have originally been a distinct race from white persons.[30] Moreover, given the existence of chattel slavery and the decimation of Native peoples, Gossett's supposition—that most whites affirmed the potential of all races—must be challenged or, at the very least, recognized as illuminating the pivotal role, even direct causal relationship of the Christian mind-set in the dehumanization of other peoples and the emergence of the "superior" white race. Unfortunately, Jefferson's speculation would become a more widely accepted fact in the nineteenth century when "racial theory explaining inherent inferiority and superiority would make great inroads not merely in popular thought but also in that of the scientists and scholars."[31]

Consequently, in the nineteenth century, the debate turned to the question of whether the races represent different species, not merely varieties of the same species. In the United States, scientists held this multispecies view or "polygenic" theory in increasing numbers. For example, Dr. Samuel Morton, a well-known Philadelphia physician, concluded from his "observations" that mulattoes grew increasingly infertile from generation to generation, such that white and black must be two separate races, genetically incompatible, with "innate mental and temperamental differences."[32] Louis Aggasiz, who emigrated from Switzerland to the United States, argued that although there was one Creator, God had created distinct human species in different geographical locations, rather than as a result of external factors such as climate. Even those who supported a single race or a "monogenic" theory of human differences, such as the southern Lutheran minister and slaveholder, John Bachman, conceded that it did not mean the other groups were equal to whites.[33] Basing his position not on scientific analysis but Scripture, Bachman argued that the "Curse of Ham" justified chattel slavery.

The so-called Curse of Ham as an oft-cited justification for slavery has been well documented.[34] Essentially, this myth represented Africans as the descendants of Noah's son Ham, who inappropriately witnessed his father lying drunken and naked in his tent. Ham's son Canaan was the bearer of the curse, which proclaimed Canaan would be the "lowest of slaves" (Gen. 9:25). These biblical verses became a long-standing proslavery apologia among Southern slaveholders, and as Stephen Haynes demonstrates, often without reference to the interpretative and exegetical traditions, which were simply posited as a given. Questions such as how Canaan became black, why Noah's sin was not punished, and why the generation beyond Ham incurred God's wrath were left unexamined by many white Americans for whom the Word of God was inerrant in its decree of the God-mandated enslavement of persons of African descent.

In sum, during the period leading up to the Civil War, racist discourse and practice questioned the very humanity of persons who were not white and presented rationales to reinforce the position of the white colonizers. Whether biblically or scientifically based, debates centered around whether Native Americans and slaves wrested from the African continent were of the same species as white people and, if so, whether they were equally human or not. The Naturalization Law of 1790 afforded citizenship only to free *white* men, despite or because of the fundamental importance of red land and black labor to the nation's economic development. The roots of white supremacy were thus planted deeply within the Christian nation from the founding of the first white settlements, despite the fact that they were not actually the "discoverers" of this long-inhabited territory. The Naturalization Act of 1790, which restricted citizenship to white people, would remain largely in effect until 1952 when racial discrimination was prohibited, as Congress removed the restriction.[35]

From the Civil War to Civil Rights

As the debate over slavery erupted into the Civil War, the vast majority of Native Americans from the southern and southeastern

United States had been resettled west of the Mississippi. Now tribes located in California and the Pacific Northwest struggled to survive following the discovery of gold in 1849, as white Americans massacred Native peoples in search of undiscovered riches buried deep within Native peoples' sacred lands. Clearly, the "Indian problem" was not resolved in the minds of white Americans. Because the Native population had moved west, the "Indian wars" of the nineteenth century also moved west. The Great Plains experienced "virtually constant war for almost 50 years" up through the Wounded Knee Massacre in the winter of 1890.[36] In 1864, for example, some 150 innocent Cheyenne were massacred at Sand Creek by troops led by Colonel John Chivington, a Methodist minister. Massacres in California led to tribal genocide. In one documented case, the Yahi Yana tribe was systematically destroyed in the 1860s. A few persons escaped annihilation, and eventually, in 1911, the sole surviving member of the tribe was "discovered" on former tribal lands. He was taken to live at the Museum of the University of California under the charge of a professor until his death four-and-a-half years later.

Alongside the strategy of genocide, the white society attempted to splinter the cohesion of the remaining tribes and further the goal of either assimilation into white culture or annihilation. The General Allotment Act of 1887, as amended by the Dawes Act of 1891, authorized the United States president to award tribal lands to individual Native Americans.[37] Those who received allotments or who resided apart from tribes, thereby modeling their lives on the white culture, also were to receive the right to citizenship. These provisions "produced a further deterioration of American Indian economies, societies, and cultures."[38] Treaties between the government and various tribes were mostly broken or left unfulfilled, especially if the government was to provide money or resources to the tribe. Just after the Civil War ended, a congressional special commission, the "Doolittle Committee" investigated the decline in the Native population. The report identified various causes of depopulation, the "aggressions of lawless white men," the loss of traditional "hunting grounds and . . . destruction of game," and the desire of white men for gold and fertile land.[39] But the commission's ultimate conclusion was that the problem "can never be remedied until the Indian race is civilized or shall entirely disappear."[40]

Although Native Americans were granted the right to vote in 1924, "citizenship . . . did little to improve the many economic and political problems the Indians faced."[41] The loss of land, which tribes considered to be sacred and integral to their cultures, the loss of hunting grounds and agricultural practices, the significant depopulation, and the desire of the federal government to reduce the strength of tribal organizations, placed Native peoples in a precarious position. In 1870, and again in 1890, two revitalization movements known as "Ghost Dances" arose. As religious rituals, Ghost Dances served to rekindle traditional beliefs and practices, while offering the hope of life and freedom for the First Peoples. These subversive rites sought to reclaim and encourage their full humanity with the hope of restoration. But the white Christian population felt threatened by these "heathen" rituals and determined to eliminate them by force. Military troops were dispatched to quell Ghost Dances, which culminated in the 1890 Wounded Knee Massacre of some three hundred Sioux, mostly women and children.[42]

Later legislation did little to protect Native Americans from racism. Following a short-lived Indian Reorganization Act of 1934, which aimed to revitalize tribal governments, the Hoover Commission of 1949 recommended the complete assimilation of Native peoples into white America.[43] In 1968, Congress passed the Indian Civil Rights Act, which protects the constitutional rights of Native Americans from discrimination by tribal authorities. The law "authorizes federal courts to intervene in *intratribal* disputes and overrule decisions made by tribal officials."[44] It was not designed to protect the rights and liberties of Native Americans against other forms or sources of discrimination. It certainly does not account for or rectify the long history of broken treaties between the US government and various tribes or the confiscated lands and destruction of life and property wrought by white Americans.

Meanwhile, for African Americans, the Civil War meant an end to slavery, which was abolished by the Thirteenth Amendment to the Constitution. Emancipation meant freedom, so it seemed, and the Fourteenth Amendment guaranteed equal protection under the law to African Americans. Shortly thereafter, the Fifteenth Amendment (1870) provided the right to vote. Yet, legal protections did not mean that freedom, equality, or full humanity was achieved. Indeed, Abraham Lincoln, whom history today rightly designates as instrumental in manumission, made clear his preference for the colonization of black Americans as both a strategy to engender white support for emancipation and the long-term solution to the nation's racial problem. Congress had appropriated funds to colonize emancipated slaves, and although Lincoln did not believe all African Americans could be colonized, he hoped his public advocacy would bolster white support for the Emancipation Proclamation. In addressing prominent members of the black community of the District of Columbia about this proposal for a colony in Central America, Lincoln reasoned:

> You and we are different races. We have between us a broader difference than exists between almost any other two races. Whether it is right or wrong I need not discuss, but this physical difference is a great disadvantage to us both, as I think your race suffer very greatly, many of them by living among us, while ours suffer from your presence. In a word we suffer on each side. If this is admitted, it affords a reason at least why we should be separated.[45]

The African American leaders expressed outrage at the President's proposal.[46] Lincoln's words demonstrate that even Americans in the Northern states did not support full integration and, in fact, Lincoln noted in his remarks that the cessation of slavery did not mean the freed slaves would be equal to the white race. Lincoln navigated the complexities of racist discourse and practice in his pursuit of preserving the nation and dismantling slavery, but understood that the elimination of racism was unrealistic. Racist discourse and practice is always stubborn in its hold and reinvents itself when forced to change.

Despite equality, freedom, and full humanity (at least for black men) in the eyes of the law, white Americans maintained the inferiority of black Americans, and the "Jim Crow" era began. Separate but equal was the order of the day in the South, though extralegal forms of segregation were also common in Northern states. Disenfranchisement through poll taxes and literacy tests, limited opportunities for employment, and other measures continued to dehumanize and, in the case of lynching, terrorize and annihilate black Americans. The law upheld the idea of separate but equal in *Plessy v. Ferguson* (1896), when the Supreme Court, in effect, established that political rights and societal discrimination are two distinct concerns.

These policies set the stage for the civil rights movement and the ongoing quest for freedom and fully human existence. After *Brown v. The Board of Education* struck down school segregation in 1954, the Civil Rights Act of 1964 and the Voting Rights Act of 1965 further dismantled the Jim Crow South. The Civil Rights Act provided a wide range of protections against discrimination and segregation. Legally, the discriminatory practices of the past century were eliminated, but of course, laws do not change attitudes or the subtleties of institutions and structures that continue to privilege and empower white Americans. By the late 1960s, both Native Americans and African Americans had been given a wide measure of legal rights and protections, yet their disadvantaged place in American society would not be eliminated. As Noll reminds us, with the exception of "African Americans and a very few white Americans, [the Civil War] never became a war to overcome racism."[47]

While Native Americans and African Americans found some measure of success in gaining legal rights, other minoritized racial and ethnic groups were struggling against the forces of white supremacy and its dehumanizing agenda. Irish immigrants, fleeing famine, settled in the northern states and began to compete for the same jobs as African Americans. The Irish had long been considered "savages" and non-white by the English, and in America they were compared unfavorably to black persons. Takaki quotes a sermon from Boston minister Theodore Parker who "claimed that some people were 'inferior in nature, some perhaps only behind us in development' on 'a lower form in the great school of Providence—negroes, Indians, Mexicans, Irish, and the like.' "[48] The Irish, who were competing with blacks for employment now sought to become "white" by assimilating into the American culture, including adopting the white supremacist discourse and practice that dehumanized and condemned African Americans. Becoming "white" was a strategy that would prove successful in gaining access to the privileges of the majority culture.

Another strategy for the Irish in their quest to become white was to serve in the army during the war against Mexico.[49] The proximity of Mexicans provided yet another test for whiteness, as "civilization" and Manifest Destiny advanced westward, even as the Civil War loomed in the near future.[50] As with the Native Americans, the insatiable desire of white Americans for land erupted in aggression against Mexico under the guise of God's providential guidance. The territory of Tejas was the focal point for the War with Mexico (1846–1848) due to the incursion of whites from the United States who established settlements on Mexican land. In the decade between 1825 and 1835, the population of white settlers plus their black slaves in Tejas ballooned from around 1,500 to some 20,000.[51] In 1835, by contrast, there were only, perhaps, 4,000 Mexicans in the territory.[52] Although in 1830 the Mexican government made slavery illegal and banned further immigration into Tejas from the United States, as Takaki insightfully suggests, "Americans continued to cross the border as illegal aliens."[53]

Though Mexico had gained independence from its European colonizers, it had also adopted their Catholic faith in large measure, such that "Christianizing the heathens" could not serve as justification for conquest by the United States. Instead, the doctrine of Manifest Destiny first posited in John O'Sullivan's essay, "Annexation," and then in a newspaper column echoing the ideology, provided the overarching thematic for this incursion, obscuring or validating the pragmatic benefits of the Mexican land to the economic development of the United States. Manifest Destiny was not framed as a legal but a moral imperative for America, since America was a white democratic nation chosen by God and vested with Anglo-Saxon superiority. To be sure, there were opponents of the doctrine of Manifest Destiny, including white opponents especially in the Northeast, but their objections did not prevail.

The Battle of the Alamo was, in fact, an armed insurrection instigated by settlers, even illegal ones, within the national borders of Mexico. It resulted in the declaration of Texas's independence from Mexico, and the Lone Star, according to Sam Houston, became a symbol of the "glory" of the Anglo-Saxon race and the defeat of Mexican "tyranny."[54] Acquiring the territory of Texas presumably fueled the ideology of Manifest Destiny, as the United States would soon justify its acquisition by force of other Mexican territories. Mexico's military was no match for the burgeoning hard power of the United States. The Treaty of Guadalupe Hidalgo ended the conflict, as Mexico ceded around forty percent, some five hundred thousand square miles, of its territory to the United States, including the present day states of Arizona, California, Colorado, Nevada, New Mexico, and Utah, in addition to Texas. Altogether, the divine mission of the United States resulted in the appropriation of more than one million square miles or 50 percent of Mexico.[55] This acquisition further fueled the economic expansion of the United States at the expense of the development of the Mexican nation. Ultimately, despite the rhetoric of Manifest Destiny and divine provision, the question remains: Was it a matter of God's will or of unholy greed wrapped in a thin mantle of theological justification?

What became of the Mexicans who now found themselves foreigners or outsiders within the borders of the United States casts further light on the logic of white supremacy. Although, under the terms of the Treaty, Mexicans (not including native, indigenous peoples) who chose to remain in the territories now under the possession of the United States were to be accorded the full rights of citizens, the reality proved to be otherwise. Lands owned by Mexican Americans were routinely confiscated by the United States without consent or acquired by white Americans through legal and economic means with which the Mexican Americans lacked familiarity. At times, United States lawyers, hired by Mexicans to defend their property rights, took advantage of their clients' lack of knowledge to the advantage of the United States. During the Jim Crow era, Mexicans Americans shared the ignominy of African Americans in terms of public access and employment opportunities. The United States economy depended upon Mexicans to cultivate cotton, construct irrigation systems, lay railroad tracks, and mine precious ores, yet Mexican laborers were routinely paid lower wages than Anglo laborers doing identical work. They, like some of their Anglo counterparts, often found themselves indebted to company towns and stores, not unlike the plantation system that dehumanized African Americans after the Civil War, so as to undermine their opportunities for education, financial stability, or employment advancement. Despite prevailing stereotypes, Mexican American laborers sometimes mobilized to strike for better wages and working conditions, as they reasserted their humanity and God-given rights and resisted white supremacy.

In the early part of the twentieth century, Mexican immigration increased as the United States required laborers for the fields, service occupations, and railroad construction. Takaki notes that in "Los Angeles, 70 percent of the Mexicans were unskilled blue-collar workers in 1918, compared to only 6 percent for Anglos" and in 1928, "a Texas official estimated that Mexicans represented about 75 percent of all construction labor in the state."[56] There was a growing racial stratification, as Mexicans were systematically barred from professional or managerial occupations. Simultaneously and ironically, a pervasive sense of alarm at the numbers of Mexicans settling in the Southwest arose that "seemed to be endangering America's cultural identity. Vanderbilt University economics professor Roy Garis urged white Americans to guard against the 'Mexicanization' of the Southwest."[57]

Already in the early twentieth century, a pattern was developing in which the southwestern states depended upon brown labor, but sought to maintain the normativity of whiteness. During World War II, the United States government recruited, even paid transportation for guest laborers from Mexico by the thousands to work the fields while Mexican Americans populated the defense industries. Mexican American women were employed as riveters on airplane assembly lines alongside women of different races and ethnicities. Mexican Americans also served in the Armed Forces, recognizing it as a path to inclusion. Still, neither service to the nation at war nor their Christian faith made Mexican Americans worthy of being deemed fully human by the majority culture, as they lacked the basic qualification of European or Anglo American whiteness. Returning from fighting fascists overseas, many Mexican American veterans discovered the war at home persisted. Having served his nation with honor, military veteran Cesar Chavez, for example, found himself confronted with the duplicity of white supremacy and thus felt compelled to initiate his crusade for the rights of farm workers.[58] It bears mentioning, as well, that Native Americans who had once been punished for using their languages contributed significantly to allied victory in World War II as Code Talkers, only to return home to society's racist discourse and practice.

The dehumanization of persons of color by white society continued to the western shores of the nation with dreams of crossing the Pacific to civilize and Christianize East Asia. Japanese, Chinese, Filipino, and other immigrants from Asia arrived in United States territory lured by the promises of American democracy, freedom, and economic opportunity. Chinese immigrants first arrived in the middle of the nineteenth century, driven by unrest and famine in China. Mostly men, these immigrants joined the gold rush with dreams of riches, but soon found themselves subject to discriminatory practices such as foreign miners' taxes. "By 1970, California had collected five million dollars from the Chinese, a sum representing between 25 to 50 percent of all state revenue."[59] Of course, no road to citizenship existed for the Chinese, who could have cried, "No taxation without representation." Chinese men also emerged as the primary labor for the Central Pacific Railroad, since white workers not only required wages, but room and board as well.[60] As was true of the Mexicans, Chinese laborers were relegated to blue collar jobs: "What enabled businessmen . . . to degrade the Chinese into a subservient laboring caste was the dominant ideology that defined America as a racially homogeneous society and Americans as white."[61] Yet, despite the preference for cheap Chinese labor, their soaring numbers led President Rutherford B. Hayes to declare a growing Chinese problem, and in 1882 the Chinese Exclusionary Act prohibited further Chinese immigration. Takaki surmises that the "[r]estriction was rooted in racism" since according to the demographics of 1880, the Chinese "constituted a mere .002 percent of the U.S. population."[62] In actuality, an economic downturn preceded the prohibition on immigration, and the prohibition thereby ensured white employment rates remained steady.

Japanese men and women immigrated at the end of the nineteenth century, first to Hawaii to work on plantations, and then to California. Their experience in the United States mirrored, in many respects, that of the Chinese in relationship to the majority white population, with one significant exception. After the bombing of Pearl Harbor, Japanese Americans on the West Coast of the contiguous forty-eight states were relocated to internment camps, forced to leave behind their property, lives, and freedom. Many of the people interned were citizens of the United States. Ironically but not surprisingly, because the Japanese Americans in Hawaii were so crucial to the islands' agricultural economy and so necessary for the rebuilding of Pearl Harbor, they remained free, despite the fact that the Japanese Americans living in Hawaii outnumbered those on the West Coast.[63]

Throughout the era leading up to the enactment of civil rights, persons of color were systematically deprived of political and economic opportunity, legally inscribed as inferior, and repeatedly denied the right to own and retain land and property, despite their significant investment in the economic development of the United States and in military service. Driving this racial logic was the justifying ideology of Manifest Destiny, which professed the innate superiority of the white (Anglo-Saxon and European) race and its God-given mission to civilize the land from coast to coast, thereby creating a glorious American Empire. Although theology and the church contributed to the ideological foundations of the superiority of the white race, there were also voices that questioned Manifest Destiny and white supremacy and offered counter or subversive narratives. The "Master Narrative" might attempt to hide the alternative narratives in order to consolidate and reinforce the power of Constantinian Christianity, but the nation, including white Americans, has never been univocal on the question of race or Christianity's commitment to fully human existence.

In *God and Race in American Politics*, Noll theorizes a Calvinist "template," framed not denominationally, but in terms of "the activist ethos bequeathed by the broadly Puritan-evangelical-Methodist voluntary pattern" for the public function of Christianity. Drawing on the writings of André Siegfried and Alexis de Tocqueville, Noll points to a sense of "mission," not only toward individual believers but also the purity of the state.[64] This ethos predisposes Americans to employ biblical arguments in public debates, most notably in relationship to the persistence of slavery, but also to "Indian rights, temperance reform, and—most significantly, civil rights."[65] Clearly, the application of biblical texts to moral and political issues has provided the appearance of divine justification no matter the position, thereby suggesting the imperative to assess that use in relation to other dynamics, notably privilege and economics.

Nonetheless, a hermeneutic of suspicion and careful attention to counter narratives can assist with the identification of Constantinian Christian impulses. Given that the question of slavery was more fundamentally a question of race and racism, Noll cites Frederick Douglass who exposed the hermeneutical moves at work:

> Nobody at the North, we think, would defend Slavery, even from the Bible, but for this color distinction. . . . Color makes all the difference in the application of our American Christianity. . . . The same book which is full of the Gospel of Liberty to one race, is crowded with arguments in justification of the slavery of another.[66]

After the Civil War, black intellectuals who questioned the white interpretations of Scripture and white expressions of Christianity began to arise in ever greater numbers, providing diverse perspectives on the relationship of the church and theology to racism, including Bishop Henry McNeal Turner, W. E. B. Du Bois, Malcolm X, and Martin Luther King Jr. The Protestant church, having itself experienced schism over the institution of slavery, certainly could not provide the moral compass or theological insight to dismantle racist discourse and practice across the nation, let alone within its own sanctuaries.

Noll provides evidence that throughout the United States, both North and South, Christians either perpetuated racist institutions or remained mute: "Historians have demonstrated that religion, in the North as well as the South, was critical in the process that brought Reconstruction to a close, restored white racist regimes to power, and turned the attention of the North away from defending citizens' rights for all."[67] More extreme Southern white Christians continued to preach the superiority of the white race and either refused to recognize constitutional equality and rights or circumvented them, most horrifically expressed in the crime of lynching as a spectator sport. Moderates became silent. Whether evangelical, such as D. L. Moody, who turned inward to personal religious experience and away from social commitments or progressive, like William Jennings Bryan, who upheld Christian commitments to social justice, racial matters were virtually eliminated from Christian discourse and practice during this era.

Horace Bushnell, perhaps the best known Protestant theologian in America in the nineteenth century, provides a glimpse into the mindset of white America. "Bushnell," writes Gossett, "argued that there were two methods by which the kingdom of God was being extended. One was the process of conversion of the heathen. The other was the expansion of Christian peoples into the four corners of the earth."[68] Bushnell even pondered whether the divine plan was to populate the world with "better and finer" people given the evidence before him, though he acknowledged that, ultimately, the matter remained in God's hand.[69]

Even the Social Gospel Movement falls short in respect to attending to racist discourse and practice. The rise of Social Darwinism meant that new claims to the superiority of the white race were posited on scientific grounds. Social Gospel adherents such as Walter Rauschenbush and Josiah Strong realized the theory of evolution, whatever its merits, could be used to exploit weaker members of society. Yet, as Gossett records, "The Social Gospel clergymen spoke out much more strongly in the area of specific economic injustices—the abuse of the laboring class in unhealthful working conditions, long hours, and poor wages, for example—than they did on matters of racial injustice."[70] He goes on to suggest that the widespread acceptance of racial inequality by evolutionary theorists made it difficult for clergy to argue against the scientists. Strong went so far as to argue that the disappearance of Native Americans was "the reflection of the will of God in preparing the land for a better race, the Anglo-Saxons."[71] Gossett concludes, "Just as Strong was able to reconcile the theory of evolution, the struggle for existence, and the survival of the fittest with an optimistic Protestant theology, so he was able to view the ascendancy and decline of races as part of the providence of God."[72]

In Strong and Bushnell, who are representative of their day rather than anomalous, white theology provided justification for the superiority of the white race by means of incorporating evolutionary theory. While often viewing other races in a "kindly" or paternalistic manner, they concluded that it was quite probable that the inferior races would eventually disappear from the earth. In the meantime, the imperative to Christianize the world remained. Moreover, the thread of Manifest Destiny was woven into the fabric of their theology. God had not only chosen the white race, but had chosen the United States and its Protestantism to fulfill the divine mission in the world.

Racism in the Aftermath of Civil Rights

Following civil rights legislation and into the twenty-first century, a new form of racial discourse, which continues to limit the freedom and humanity of people of color can be identified. Central to this reinscribed racism is the reality—observed in previous eras—that legislation does not function so as to reshape attitudes, ideologies, or theological convictions. Sociologists refer to this new racism as "modern racism," "color-blind racism," and "racial realism," among other designations. The advent of the Obama presidency highlighted the nature of contemporary racial discourse within the United States. Following President Obama's election, some pundits proposed that his presidency symbolized the United States had entered a "post-racial" age. Yet, the reality of life in the United States, objectively assessed and in degrees or gradations of racism rather than an either-or logic, suggests anything but a post-racial society. While Obama's presidency is a historic moment, it should not be presented as proof that racism is overcome. While it might indicate that some forms of racism have been eliminated or reinvented, it may not even symbolize a moment in which racialized discourse and practice—defined as that which uncovers, analyzes, and dismantles racism—has come of age.

Most, if not all persons of color in the United States have experienced the systemic racism embedded in contemporary society. Discriminatory practices in lending, employment, housing, and a host of other areas persist. For example, during the economic downturn of 2009, unemployment statistics consistently demonstrated that African Americans experience higher rates of unemployment than do whites. More recent Bureau of Labors statistics confirm that blacks are almost twice as likely to be unemployed than white workers.[73] Statistics compiled by The Sentencing Project demonstrate that the odds of a person going to prison in the United States are nearly six times higher for African Americans than white Americans and Hispanics are incarcerated at double the rate for whites.[74] Persons of color routinely receive harsher sentences than white Americans who commit equivalent crimes. Similarly, Native Americans, in the words of Stephen Pevar, "are the most disadvantaged people in our society." He explains:

> They have the lowest life expectancy, living only two-thirds as long as whites. Indians also suffer from an unemployment rate of nearly 45 percent, about ten times the national average. . . . Nearly one-third of Indian

households live below the poverty level, a number twice as high as the white population, and on some reservations, the poverty rate approaches 65 percent.[75]

Many more statistics and narratives could support the wide disparities in the quality of life, access to resources, and freedom of opportunities experienced by persons of color in the United States when compared to white Americans. Even in an economy where increasing numbers of white Americans are joining the ranks of unemployed, underemployed, and impoverished, the percentages of persons of color in those categories grows proportionately. As Derrick Bell described, "Black people are the magical faces at the bottom of society's well. Even the poorest whites, those who must live their lives only a few levels above, gain their self-esteem by gazing down."[76] Other people of color understand how the white faces gaze downward at them as well, even as they sometimes join in the sin of comparatives by arguing they are above blacks on the racial hierarchy. Yet, consistent with Foucault's claim regarding the emotional nature of racial discourses, statistics and hard data do little to convince white Americans that discriminatory practices and racist systems and structures continue to affect the life and well-being of persons of color, despite legal protections. There exists a large and growing body of sociological literature on this phenomenon, variously labeled as "modern racism" (Merenstein), "color-blind racism" (Bonilla-Silva), and "racial realism" (Brown et al), among others.

This contemporary racial discourse is marked by a few central assumptions. First, civil rights legislation was successful and racial inequalities have been eliminated, though some *individual* acts of racism still occur. Second, any policies related to equal and fair treatment are now unnecessary, since the playing field has been leveled. Third, any lack of success within the United States is attributed to the failure of racial groups to take advantage of the opportunities that exist. Cultural characteristics, as well as a persistent "victim" mentality, are deemed responsible for this failure. Consequently, while it is true that overt forms of racism such as slavery, Jim Crow laws, and boarding schools for tribal children are a thing of the past, subtle and covert forms of racism embedded in institutional and social practices continue to dehumanize and limit the possibilities and the fullness of life for persons of color. As Bell argues, "the very absence of visible signs of discrimination creates an atmosphere of racial neutrality and encourages whites to believe that racism is a thing of the past."[77] White theology apparently subscribes to this dictum with its silence and supposed neutrality.

In an insightful study, Merenstein demonstrates that immigrants quickly learn the racist discourse and practice of the United States and recognize the hierarchical ordering in which white Americans are on top and African Americans on the bottom.[78] In other words, the darker the skin, the lower one's place in the hierarchy. Immigrants then strategize to secure their place somewhere within this hierarchy, pushing against the identification as "black," while reciting the narrative that through sheer hard work the "American Dream" is possible for anyone. Racist discourse is learned and reinvents itself, such that racism persists. Despite hard evidence of the racism that is systemically present in American society, contemporary discourse, including theological discourse, discounts and denies its pervasiveness. Hence, white Americans can remain unaware of the institutional practices and power arrangements that reinforce white privilege and racial inequalities. Racial identity becomes irrelevant in the eyes of the majority white culture, even as white Americans benefit from the ongoing arrangements. Contemporary racism largely reproduces the original discourses of subhuman or inferior races, as it discounts any long-term effects accruing to the four hundred years of discrimination and debilitation at the hands of white America and blames "racial" characteristics for pervasive inequities. Harping on individual rights and responsibilities, white Americans and Christians ignore the existence of systemic sin as it undermines right relationship to God and others. Freedom remains elusive for persons who do not meet the standard of "whiteness." The quest for fully human existence remains a priority for people of color, while substantial numbers of white Americans, including many Christians, believe that we need no longer attend to racism beyond isolated, individual instances of moral failure.

Although theologians and ecclesial bodies are more aware than ever of the history of racism within and beyond the church, Sunday morning continues to be the most segregated time of the week across the United States. Statistical evidence supports the claim that the Christian church is slow to change and remains predominantly white. In 2010, the United States Census reported that 72.4 percent of the US population identify as members of the white race. This figure includes those who report themselves as ethnically "Hispanic or Latino." Thus, the "white, non-Hispanic" population composes 64 percent of the total population, a proportional decrease of 5 percent from the 2000 census. The census reported the following racial categories as a percentage of the total population: "Black/African American" at 12.6 percent,

"Asian" at 4.8 percent, "American Indian and Native Alaskan" at 0.9 percent, "Native Hawaiian and Other Pacific Islander" at 0.2 percent, "Some Other Race" at 6.2 percent, and "Two or More Races" at 2.9 percent. Those who identify as being of Hispanic or Latino origin represent 16.3 percent of the total population.[79]

If we compare these figures with 2009 data collected in the "U.S. Religious Landscape Survey" conducted by the Pew Forum on Religion and Public Life, the racial composition of the Christian churches does not come close to resembling the general population, with the exception of Catholicism: Evangelical Protestant churches are 81 percent white (non-Hispanic), Mainline Protestant 91 percent, Orthodox 87 percent, Other Christians 77 percent, and Catholics 65 percent (29 percent of Catholic membership is Hispanic).[80] The racial composition of faculty in theological schools in the United States is even less representative of the general population. White faculty members at all ranks compose 81 percent of the total, black faculty members 7.8 percent, Latino/as 3.6 percent, Asian and Pacific Islanders 5.6 percent, American Indians and Alaska Natives 0.1 percent, multiracial 0.2 percent, and visa/non-resident aliens 0.8 percent.[81] In sum, these data suggest that both the churches and seminaries remain predominantly white and lag behind the general population in terms of racial diversity. Indeed, the concern for "inclusion" within churches and theological schools seldom focuses on systemic institutional change aimed at decentering white privilege and dismantling white supremacy. Rather, "hospitality" is lifted up as an essential Christian attitude, thereby enabling whiteness to remain the center of power that "welcomes" others into the space, but on its own terms. Mutual transformation is thwarted if unacknowledged, invisible systemic racism continues to provide the shape and content of the communal life.

Given this history and contemporary manifestation of racist discourse and practice, where are the white theologians who provide critical appraisal of the function, nature, and power of white privilege and white supremacy? As we noted in the previous chapter, white theologians remain silent, in large measure, and are unwilling or unable to enter into racialized discourse and practice as a necessary component of theological discourse in the United States. Theologians of color continue to articulate conceptions of fully human existence within the context of the United States and its long history of racism. But white theologians appear little interested in joining the conversation. Perhaps the history of theological justification for racism, Manifest Destiny, and dehumanization has resulted in an era of extreme caution. Perhaps it is a reflection of the overarching sense of racial "neutrality" held by many white Americans today as most reflective of a loving disposition. Perhaps it is a marker of racism so deeply embedded in the white world view that theologians actually believe they demonstrate a commitment to racial justice and equality that need not be named in theological writings. Whatever the rationale, white theologians are faced with an opportunity to shape the next era of racial history in the United States and, as a result, to reform and renew the Christian churches. In the concluding chapter, we will examine the contours of this theological aperture and present a challenge to theologians; in particular, white theologians.

4

REFORMATION

Demography is redefining who is an American. The time has come for us to embrace our varied selves. A new America is approaching.
—Ronald Takaki

No story or song will translate the full impact of falling, or the inverse power of rising up.
—Joy Harjo

Christ has died, Christ is risen, Christ will come again.

Interpretations of the Great Commission of Matthew 28:18-20 have long provided the justification and framework for the Christianization of the world, a logic intertwined with racist discourse and practice for most of the history of the United States. Sanctioning economic development and wars in the name of Christianizing the "heathens," the Great Commission helped fuel the ideology of Manifest Destiny and the decimation of persons of color who alternately proved useful and disposable to the majority white culture and its version of Constantinian Christianity. Although the words of Jesus in the Gospel of Matthew, indeed, command his followers to "make disciples of all nations, baptizing them in the name of the Father and of the Son and of the Holy Spirit," the verses have a long history of misuse, to include providing justification for slavery, the appropriation of indigenous tribal lands, and the war against Mexico, to name a few examples. In the wrong hands, the Bible remains a dangerous weapon that can serve and has served very human purposes such as greed, power, and domination. In the same Matthew passage, Jesus also indicates that we should teach others "to obey everything that I have commanded you," yet those who diminish the lives of others fail to be obedient in the primary commandment to love God and our neighbor as ourselves.

Of course, the Bible also remains one of the most powerful sources of the transforming love and justice that engenders life abundant, when we allow ourselves to receive and participate in the grace of God. To go out to others with the love of Christ means not to insist upon our own human way, but rather to encounter others through mutual dialogue and tangible acts that enable the flourishing of life—not simply spiritual life, but the life of the whole person in all its dimensions. The command of Matthew 28 becomes clearer in dialogue with Matthew 25, which suggests the gospel is about food, clothing, welcome to the stranger, the eradication of disease, and release from prison. Rather than drawing others into the center we occupy to remake them in our image, we are commanded to go out into places where we, ourselves, might encounter God's creation in mutually transformative ways. Through the eyes of faith, we learn to see the image of God stamped upon each human being. Through sharing the love of Christ in tangible and concrete material expressions, others may also receive the gift of grace and thereby choose to allow the fullness of the *imago Dei* to be realized within their own lives. Fully human existence is always a function of grace in cooperation with our response to God's initiative.

In the preceding chapters we have argued that the theological task must include attention to racialized discourse and practice as a means of uncovering, analyzing, and dismantling racist discourse and practice that undermines the full humanity of persons of color and white persons who participate in systemic sin. In this systemic diminishment of life, Christians fail to proclaim and participate in the life-furthering gospel of Jesus Christ. Racialized discourse and practice also serves as a corrective to silence and neutrality, which are too often posited as appropriate theological stances, even as they reinforce and reinscribe racism in theology, the church, and the larger society. Racialized discourse and practice, as a methodology or a necessary theological task, provides a means to challenge the systemic dehumanization of persons of color in the United States. It can serve as a means of grace for the renewal of the church and the transformation of the world as it names the reality in which we live and participate apart from or in opposition to the divine promise of life abundant.

We began by describing the nature and function of Constantinian Christianity which, in its American form, incorporates not only economics, politics, power, and Christianity, but also white supremacy as a system constructed by white people to the advantage of white people. Theologies that reinforce the systemic advantages and objectives of Constantinian Christianity can be named as "theologies of privilege," in which speaking truth to power is discouraged, since to do so would undermine one's own position and access to resources and opportunities. Theologies of privilege may claim to express love toward all persons and to despise racism, yet the discourse and practice emerging from these theologies often belie their stated intentions in small or greater ways. The theology of Peter Hodgson might be illustrative of how theologies of privilege incorporate the logic of white supremacy under the auspices of promoting freedom and fully human existence, despite his good intentions. Most introductory textbooks written by white theologians share the same fate. Theologies of privilege enter into a symbiotic relationship with Constantinian Christianity such that, in the case of racism, they contribute to discourse and practice that enable the discriminatory structures to be reinvented and reinscribed in each new era. Both progressive and conservative theologies have been guilty of complicity with Constantinian Christianity, as self-preservation and protection of privileges can be found at both ends of the theological spectrum, as well as in the moderate middle.

Whether consciously or not, theologies of privilege perpetuate the system of privileges, of white supremacy, accruing to the elites or substantive power holders, and this logic spreads from top to bottom of the racial hierarchy until the faces at the bottom of the well have no one to look down upon and must speak up. While theologies of privilege often reinforce the positions of the wealthy and of men, who have traditionally stood on the highest rungs in the United States, race has proven to be a defining and enduring source of oppression in the United States. To be a poor woman of color is to exist at the intersection of multiple sources of dehumanization, whereas a poor white woman, a poor man of color, or a rich woman of color may yet cast their gaze downward upon her. Racism provides the greatest downward leverage and, therefore, requires consciously sustained reflection and analysis. White persons always retain the power to slip back under the cloak of invisible whiteness if attending to racism becomes too difficult, painful, or threatening.

Chapter 2 furthered the goal of cultivating racialized discourse and practice as it examined theological anthropologies written by theologians of color side-by-side those of white theologians who largely pursue variations on theologies of privilege. Repeatedly, theologians of color approach the doctrine of humanity by attending to racialized discourse, naming how racism has functioned to undermine fully human existence for both oppressor and oppressed. Theologians of color also call on their communities to interrogate their own appropriation of the dominant discourse that identifies them as less than fully human. The differences in approaches between white theologians and those of color are unmistakable and should become a source of theological reflection for white theologians.

Why do we who are white hesitate to identify the ways that racism in both the church and society has undermined the flourishing of persons of color? It is not sufficient to claim that, as Christians, we love everyone the same, when systemic sin provides us with resources, opportunities, and life possibilities that are denied to others we claim to love. White theologians have an opportunity to enter into a new reformation in which racialized discourse and practice serves to awaken Christians to the systemic sin of white supremacy, to repent of past and present lovelessness toward our neighbors, and to participate in the renewal of radical relationality.

Chapter 3 delineated the periodization of racial history in the United States by analyzing the racist logic central to each era. White Americans sought to determine the nature, place, and utility or disposability of persons of color in relation to the goals of white privilege and white supremacy. The historical narrative reveals a pattern of dehumanization toward all persons of color, regardless of country of origin (including the original inhabitants of the United States) or religion (given that the requirements for Christianizing the heathens could never be satisfied for want of whiteness). Even the current era, following the enactment of civil rights legislation, has contributed to the ongoing dehumanization of persons of color by shifting to a racist discourse and practice that hides under the cloak of neutrality or the mask of colorblindness. George Lipsitz refers to this phenomenon as the "white spatial imaginary," which "promotes a self-renewing culture of denial and disavowal. It produces a debilitating refusal to recognize the role of race as a social force."[1] When the very fabric of the United States is riddled with discriminatory systems and logic, neutrality serves only to reinforce and perpetuate the ways of death and destruction, despite the claim to follow Jesus Christ.

Given the relationship of Christianity to racism in creating and sustaining economic and political privilege for white Americans, the concern for theological anthropologies that further fully human existence in relation to God and others, and the historical reinvention of racist discourse and practice, theologians are now faced with a theological aperture, an opportunity to shape the subsequent or emerging era of racial history in the United States and participate in a more just society as well as a church that more tangibly embodies the early Jesus movement and the gospel. White theologians who engage in racialized discourse and practice can enter into a process of atonement for both racism and feigned neutrality as they engender more fully human ways of being in the world and with one another. Such theological activity entails three responses or modes of restoration and three tasks of renewal and reformation.

Three Modes of Restoration

The concept of repentance is a fitting one given the historical and contemporary participation of theology in racist discourse and practice. Returning to God requires a turning of our attention, a reorientation of our attitude, a conscientization process aimed not only at developing an awareness of the complicity of theology with the nation's racist history but also a deepened understanding and appreciation of the goodness of different cultures. We must become black with God, to use the phrase of James Cone. We must become black, brown, yellow, and red with God. This mode of renewal does not propose blackness as an ontological condition, but as a theological commitment to engaging and learning from communities of color. It is a formative process of learning what it means to be human without diminishing the complexity and varieties of human community. This is not to suggest we hold a position of relativism, but rather that race, particularly normative whiteness, does not provide adequate grounds for adjudicating what is appropriately human. Also indicated is a response to the conclusion that legislation does not transform attitudes and beliefs.

White supremacy continues to provide the basic epistemological structure for normative human being in the United States, and white theologians have routinely adopted this framework, if not actively then via passive neutrality. There is no imperative or incentive for white theologians to resist white privilege and supremacy save one: the demand of the gospel of Jesus Christ, the vocation to follow the way of abundant life for all. Because the white theological tradition has been positioned as normative, persons of color have been required not only to master the white European tradition but also a second body of literature if they wish to study and engage the writings of minoritized racial and ethnic scholars. The white conscientization process thus begins with a commitment to study and incorporate into theological projects a tradition of theological literature rooted in the perspectives of at least one minoritized racial or ethnic community. In this way, a nonthreatening intellectual dialogue can begin to foster an empathetic engagement with persons of color. The purpose is to listen to voices of color and to encounter them in the presence of grace.

Although reading and even dialogue around theological writings by scholars of color can begin the conscientization process, it remains only a first step. To develop genuine empathy and mutuality requires placing one's self in communities of color where one is no longer a member of the majority culture in that location. Too often these attempts at encounter consist of one or two visits, such that the engagement with the community becomes little more than the detached observer of a spectacle or performance. No meaningful relationships are formed, and the depths of the culture remain hidden to the casual observer. Experience proves that it takes time and regular, ongoing participation if communities of color are to develop a level of trust with white people whose participation in whiteness has betrayed them and sustained dehumanizing systems. Likewise, it takes time and regular, ongoing participation for white persons to reorient their vision to recognize both their whiteness and the contours of a different racial or ethnic culture or, in the terms of Lipsitz, different racialized "spatial imaginaries."

True conscientization, becoming black with God, requires the development of the ability to see and navigate the world through both a white cultural lens and another one, a "double consciousness," described by W. E. B. Du Bois. The African American is, Du Bois explains,

> born with a veil, and gifted with second-sight in this American world,—a world which yields him no true self-consciousness, but only lets him see himself through the revelation of the other world. It is a peculiar sensation, this double-consciousness, this sense of always looking at one's self through the eyes of others, of measuring one's soul by the tape of a world that looks on in amused contempt and pity. One ever feels his twoness,—an American, a Negro; two souls, two thoughts, two unreconciled strivings; two warring ideals in one dark body, whose dogged strength alone keeps it from being torn asunder.[2]

Of course, in Du Bois's analysis, being American is equated with whiteness. Because white culture is often hidden, unnamed, and unmarked, different cultures are considered "other," even as white culture denies its own existence. This reality suggests that participation in communities of color can enable white Americans to become deeply and critically conscious of their own culture for the first time. In conversation and participation with an alternative cultural lens or spatial imaginary, the white theologian experiences the discomfort of being on the margins, becomes attuned to the cultural norms at work in the community, and can begin to discern the contours of the white culture that previously remained invisible. By the grace of God, the white theologian is gifted with new eyes, taking on the mind of Christ, and enabled to participate in blackness or redness or brownness or yellowness or any combination of hues. The development of one's double consciousness also lays the groundwork for embracing theological *mestizaje* or the notion of the mutual interplay of races and cultures and learning to inhabit two different worlds. Successfully negotiating two or more cultural perspectives can provide for a richer and more adequate theological understanding of what it means to be human in relationship to God and neighbor.

The second mode of restoration lies in the need to establish an ethical component to theological reflection. With the disciplinary division between theology proper (i.e., systematic theology) and Christian ethics, the ethicist necessarily utilizes a theological framework, but systematic theological reflection need not attend to ethical considerations, even the ethical interrogation of its own epistemological framework. Theology may express a concern for justice as theologically relevant, but it has no imperative to engage in the critical mode of interrogating its own ethical engagement or lack thereof. Illustrative is Paul Tillich's *Systematic Theology*, where he claimed that, "an 'existential' theology implies ethics in such a way that no special section for ethical theology is needed."[3] Tillich recognized the moral dilemma of racism in the United States, but despite his early concern in Germany for "religious socialism" with its attention to political and economic realities, as well as culture, he was unable to engage in racialized discourse and practice, even as he benefited from the structures of whiteness in the United States.[4] On the shores of America, Tillich became white. In the conceptual compartmentalization of theology and ethics, racialized discourse and practice with its attentiveness to exposing racism has little or no place in the construction or reconstruction of Christian doctrine.

But consciously entering into racialized discourse and practice provides both the opportunity and necessity to address this lacuna and to provide restorative momentum.

The third mode of restoration entails theological "reparations." Legally, reparations are intended to redress some wrong or to provide compensation, often financial, for systematic violations of human rights. In a similar vein, we might suggest that theological reparations seek to redress the history of white theology's complicity in the nation's racist discourse and practice. Both the conscientization process and the ethical component to theological discourse can be considered measures of redress, as they function to reveal and record the systemic nature of white privilege and white supremacy. Of course, white Americans frequently deny that systemic advantages and disadvantages exist. As Lipsitz argues:

> The white spatial imaginary is innately ahistorical. It accepts the prevailing imbalances of wealth and power between racialized spaces as a baseline reality that should not be disturbed, as an accurate register of the achievement and worth of the people who live in those spaces. If whites live in wealthy suburbs and Blacks live in impoverished ghettos, the white spatial imaginary says, it is because whites have worked hard and succeeded while Blacks have exerted too little effort and failed. The long history of rewards for racism and subsidies for segregation disappears from this equation. The wealth that whites inherit from previous generations is rarely mentioned. We do not acknowledge the cumulative vulnerabilities that Black individuals and communities face from centuries of impediments.[5]

Theological reparations, then, take seriously the idea that systemic discrimination and limitations rather than personal moral failure might be the root cause of racial disparities and discriminatory patterns. Only then does it become possible to consider and devise ways to compensate for the historical trauma and dehumanizing effects of racism. While the strategies employed by society and the church in deploying reparations can be many and varied, we will consider briefly three explicitly theological forms of reparation.

Reparations: Three Theological Tasks

Three basic theological tasks can begin to reform the racist discourse and practice of Christianity in relationship to the United States and the dehumanizing processes and systems that continue to undermine the mission of God in the world and its offer of life abundant to all. These forms of theological reparations might be described simply as: (1) a historical task, (2) an analytical task, and (3) a practical task. All three involve truth-telling or speaking truth to power in the presence of grace and the light of the gospel.

First, doing theology that engages racialized discourse and practice demands that we expose Constantinian Christianity and rekindle the prophetic tradition of the Jesus movement. A central task of theology, then, is to illuminate the perspective, conditions, and experiences of those persons who have been marginalized and dehumanized within American society, as well as those who are being dehumanized by the processes of contemporary globalization in which whiteness participates. At the same time, theology must illuminate how racism dehumanizes white Americans as well as persons of color. It is said that history is written by the victors, by the powerful, by those who ultimately dominate any particular era. Yet, salvation history, the history of God's liberating and life-furthering presence, is the history of the underside, the defeated, the humiliated, the despised, and the crucified receiving the fullness of life. The early Christians of the Jesus movement were located on the underside. Christians of every era remain the children of the poor and despised. Christians, more than most, should understand that the history of racism in the United States is a history of the powerful and privileged seeking to secure and retain their power and privilege, rather than following the way of Jesus who, in the words of Mary's Magnificat, "has brought down the powerful from their thrones" (Luke 1:52) and served not self-interest, but the mission of God in the world. Exposing Constantinian Christianity means demonstrating that, in practice, the "American way of life"—inscribed as promoting freedom, democracy, equality, Christian faith, and human life—has often dehumanized, impoverished, and used people, especially people of color, to the benefit of white Americans. Refusing to participate in Constantinian Christianity through exposing its function and recurring patterns of disenfranchisement is a historical task.

Second, doing theology in order to engage in racialized discourse and practice requires an idea of justice that moves beyond that of creating just laws and institutions. The discourse of modern racism, which claims that laws and institutions have eliminated racism even though multiple indicators suggest exactly the opposite, highlights the distinction between what Amartya Sen calls "arrangement-focused" and "realization-focused" conceptions of justice. Sen turns to classical Sanskrit to explain these different ways of viewing justice.[6] *Niti* focuses on institutional arrangements and organizational propriety. It judges the justness of institutions and rules. *Nyaya* considers "the world that actually emerges, not just the institutions or rules we happen to have."[7] In other words, *nyaya* considers the lives that people actually live as a result of those institutions and rules. Thus, if laws in the United States are intended to eliminate racism, but racism still exists in multiple forms, justice is not served. Theologically, this task serves to underscore the reality of systemic sin. Although human beings must seek to create just institutions and systems, we also acknowledge that such organizations fall short of the intended outcomes and stand in need of continual reformation. By analyzing how those arrangements actually influence human life, for good or for ill, theologians can illuminate systemic sin and reorient Christians toward practices that promote the full humanity of others. This is an analytical task.

Finally, the historical and analytical tasks point toward the third task, which is a practical one. Theologians are called to challenge the church to reform its practices whenever and wherever they are shown to be dehumanizing, and, in particular, held hostage to the insidious and seductive power of whiteness. Subsequently, the church is called to challenge the society to reform its practices whenever and wherever they are shown to be dehumanizing and held hostage to white supremacy. Yet, whenever white Americans pursue reformation, reparations, or redress in relation to minoritized racial and ethnic persons and communities, the danger of paternalism and even neocolonialism in the form of "inclusion" into the center of whiteness lies unmistakably near: White churches that open their doors to communities of color, but remain unwilling to alter even their style of worship or music. Predominantly white denominations, headquartered in the United States, which extend globally, but develop structures to limit the voting rights of the international members and to control the purse strings because the largest share of the money is collected from American pockets. Theological seminaries that profess to be inclusive but practice "tokenism" in hiring, adopt textbooks or essays by scholars of color as supplements—if at all—to the core white European tradition, and label as "bad colleagues" those who refuse to accommodate white supremacy in hiring, tenure, and promotion decisions. Many more examples could be provided, but the point is simple: inclusion from the epistemologically omniscient center of whiteness will not renew the church or lead to societal transformation.

In contrast to the logic of inclusion, theological reparations become meaningful when white theologians, theological schools, and churches collaborate with persons and communities of color on an equal basis, sharing in decision making, coming to mutual agreement, and resisting the temptation to override or proscribe the process based upon the needs, vision, impatience, or supposed knowledge of the white collaborators. If a seminary is to create a program for Native American ministerial preparation, then the shape of that program must be determined by the Native American community itself in conversation with the pragmatic realities of theological education. If a denomination is to undertake a new church start in a minoritized racial or ethnic community, it must allow the community of color to envision and design the contours of the congregation's ministry—and the overarching concern cannot be financial sustainability given the historical and ongoing deprivation of economic opportunities among communities of color. Ministry cannot allow financial considerations to dominate the transformation of lives and communities, and even the transfer of money from haves to have nots for the support of the congregation does not mean that authority and control of the community and ministry accompany the money. Ministry based primarily and centrally upon money considerations will almost always fail, since Christians cannot serve both God and mammon. Money remains one of the most powerful weapons of white supremacy in retaining its position of centrality and control and, therefore, dehumanization. Instead of placing the dollar sign before the cross, dangling it over the altar of human self-glorification, white Christians who are attuned and open to the presence of grace are able to participate in their own process of transformation and sanctification through mutual exchange and by following the Holy Spirit into unfamiliar places where they might witness unexpected manifestations. The practical theological task, which entails this messy and difficult work of mutual learning and transformation in the presence of grace, provides a path to entering into diverse spatial imaginaries and placing God, rather than whiteness or any other idol, at the center of our lives.

Repentance entails turning and returning to God's bold love as the center of human life. Reformation entails breaking open the systems, logic, epistemological shackles, and worldly priorities that derail the movement of grace as it seeks to bring abundant life to the whole of creation regardless of pigmentation or genetic configuration. What we have sketched here in the concluding chapter is merely a skeletal framework, generative in nature, intend to facilitate the engagement with racialized discourse and practice as a primary task for theology in the twenty-first century, particularly for theologians who profess to be followers of Jesus Christ, the one who resisted the temptations of power, wealth, and immortality and pursued a ministry of healing, wholeness, and life abundant for all people. There exists no map or guidebook for the theological aperture now before us. Still, it beckons us to step out by faith, to participate in blackness, redness, brownness, and yellowness and to rediscover therein the true lightness of the world.

NOTES

Introduction

Epigraph. James H. Cone, "Theology's Great Sin: Silence in the Face of White Supremacy," *Black Theology: An International Journal* 2.2 (July 2004): 142.

1. Cone, "Theology's Great Sin," 142.

2. James H. Cone, "God Is Black," in *Lift Every Voice: Constructing Christian Theologies from the Underside,* rev. ed., ed. Mary Potter Engel and Susan B. Thistlethwaite (Maryknoll, NY: Orbis Books, 1998).

3. Cone, "Theology's Great Sin," 144.

4. Of course, the nation's demographics are changing rapidly, such that within the next fifty years the white population will become a minority culture as a so-called "majority minority" will exist from coast to coast.

5. Ibid., 148.

6. Cone, "Theology's Great Sin," 149.

7. Ibid.

8. Ibid.

9. The phrase "racialized discourse and practice" is not to be interpreted in a pejorative manner. Because racism and racial discrimination exist in the United States and its public, private, and faith-based organizations, exposing the nature and manifestations of race is a necessary task. Silence will not eliminate racism. Thus, rather than silence, theology must enter a phase in which racialized discourse is engaged in order to reconstruct theology and address systemic sin. By contrast, racist discourse and practice is that which engages in the binary logic of the superiority of white people and inferiority of persons of color, whether or not such racism is explicit and overt, individual or corporate, acknowledged or denied. It functions so as to reinforce white privilege and white supremacy.

1. America's Original Sin

Epigraph. James H. Cone, "Theology's Great Sin: Silence in the Face of White Supremacy," *Black Theology: An International Journal* 2.2 (July 2004), 142.

Epigraph. James H. Cone, *The Cross and the Lynching Tree* (Maryknoll, NY: Orbis, 2011), 159.

1. To be sure, the founding of the United States excluded women and those without property from these values in addition to persons of color.

2. Granted, in earlier eras in the United States, racism was an accepted practice particularly within the majority white culture that sought justification for the subordination of other races and cultures. Subsequent chapters will explore this point further.

3. *The Oxford English Dictionary*, 3rd ed., cites the 1926 *Manchester Guardian* (England) as perhaps the earliest usage of the term. June 2008; online version September 2011, accessed October 9, 2011, http://www.oed.com/view/Entry/157097.

4. Ali Rattansi, *Racism: A Very Short Introduction* (Oxford: Oxford University Press, 2007), 95.

5. Rattansi, 107.

6. Ibid.

7. Kwame Anthony Appiah, *The Ethics of Identity* (Princeton, NJ: Princeton University Press, 2005), 65.

8. Ibid., 66.

9. Ibid., 66–69.

10. Ibid., 113.

11. "Hispanic" of course is a category of ethnicity constructed within the United States in the past forty or so years to identify Spanish-speaking persons of Latin American descent. The term "Hispanic" properly refers to persons from the Iberian Peninsula ("Hispania"). Its usage reflects the legacy of colonization, such that many persons of Latin American descent prefer to identify as "Latino" or "Latina." Even so, this nomenclature is also contested. See Miguel H. Díaz, *On Being Human* (Maryknoll, NY: Orbis Books, 2001), 8-18.

12. Appiah, *The Ethics of Identity*, 72.

13. Ibid., 91. Although political neutrality, as suggested here by Appiah, might be an appropriate goal, theological "neutrality" often functions to reinforce white privilege—a phenomenon we will consider in chapter 3.

14. Ibid., 115.

15. Appiah, *The Ethics of Identity*, 185.

16. See, for example, Beth Frankel Merenstein, *Immigrants and Modern Racism: Reproducing Inequality* (Boulder: Lynne Reinner Publishers, 2008); Eduardo Bonilla-Silva, *Racism without Racists: Color-Blind Racism and the Persistence of Racial Inequality in the United States*, 2nd ed. (Lanham, MD: Rowman & Littlefield, 2006); and Michael K. Brown et al., *White-Washing Race: The Myth of a Color-Blind Society* (Berkeley: University of California Press, 2003).

17. Peggy McIntosh, "Unpacking the Invisible Knapsack," in *White Privilege: Essential Readings on the Other Side of Racism*, 3rd ed., ed. Paula S. Rothenberg (New York: Worth Publishers, 2008), 123. See also the work of George Lipsitz. In *How Racism Takes Place*, he claims that due to "racialized space, whiteness in this society is not so much a color as a condition. It is a structured advantage that channels unfair gains and unjust enrichments to whites." (Philadelphia: Temple University Press, 2011), 3.

18. McIntosh, "Unpacking the Invisible Knapsack," 124–25.

19. Steve Garner, *Whiteness: An Introduction* (New York: Routledge, 2007), 34. Garner's claim is made in reference to Richard Dyer's study of whiteness in relation to film and photography, *White* (London: Routledge, 1997).

20. Garner, *Whiteness*, 39.

21. Charles W. Mills, "Racial Exploitation and the Wages of Whiteness," in *What White Looks Like*, ed. George Yancy (New York: Routledge, 2004), 31.

22. Joerg Rieger, *Christ and Empire* (Minneapolis: Fortress, 2007), 71.

23. Enrique Dussel, *History and the Theology of Liberation*, trans. John Drury (Maryknoll, NY: Orbis Books, 1976), 70.

24. Ibid., 71.

25. Rieger, *Christ and Empire*, 71.

26. Cornel West, *Democracy Matters* (New York: Penguin Books, 2004), 1–2.

27. Ibid., 14.

28. Ibid., 45.

29. Ibid., 150.

30. Ibid., 114.

31. Ibid., 163.

32. Joerg Rieger, *Globalization and Theology* (Nashville: Abingdon, 2010), 6.

33. Ibid.

34. The use of Christian discourse and practice to reinforce the privileges of the powerful would be a form of what Rieger describes as "soft power." See his *Globalization and Theology*.

2. Being Human

Epigraph. George D. Kelsey, *Racism and the Christian Understanding of Man* (New York: Scribner, 1965), 23. Prior to the rise of liberation theologies, Kelsey addressed racism utilizing a Tillichian method of correlation which characterized racism as an idolatrous faith system. Clearly, one need not utilize a strictly liberation theological method to take seriously the racist discourse and practice embedded within the United States.

Epigraph. Ada María Isasi-Díaz, *Mujerista Theology* (Maryknoll, NY: Orbis Books, 1996), 131.

Epigraph. Dwight N. Hopkins, *Being Human: Race, Culture, and Religion* (Minneapolis: Fortress, 2005), 188.

1. This statement does not suggest that other doctrines are not implicated in the persistence of racism. To be sure, ecclesiology, christology, and theology proper are intimately related to racist discourse and practice and its dismantling. The point here is that throughout the history of the United States, the question

or problem of fully human existence has driven the logic and expressions of racism.

2. James H. Cone, *Black Theology and Black Power* (Maryknoll, NY: Orbis Books, 1997; original ed. 1969 by Harper & Row), 11.

3. Ibid.

4. Ibid., 49.

5. Ibid., 52.

6. Ibid., 53

7. Ibid., 56.

8. Ibid., 42.

9. James H. Cone, *The Cross and the Lynching Tree* (Maryknoll, NY: Orbis, 2011), 154.

10. Ibid., xviii.

11. Rubén Rosario Rodríguez, *Racism and God-Talk: A Latino/a Perspective* (New York: New York University Press, 2008), 11.

12. Ibid., 15.

13. Ibid., 238.

14. My thanks to Dr. Jeannette Rodríguez for recommending Miguel Díaz's *investigación*.

15. Miguel H. Díaz, *On Being Human* (Maryknoll, NY: Orbis Books, 2001), xiv.

16. Ibid., 2.

17. Ibid., 13.

18. Ibid., 14.

19. Ibid., 15.

20. Ibid., 56.

21. See also George Kelsey's *Racism and the Christian Understanding of Man*, which utilizes a Tillichian method of correlation. Essays in *Beyond the Pale: Reading Theology from the Margins*, ed. Stacey M. Floyd-Thomas and Miguel De La Torre (Louisville: Westminister John Knox , 2011) provide further evidence of this claim.

22. Hopkins, *Being Human*, 4.

23. Ibid., 119.

24. Ibid.

25. Ibid., 130.

26. Stacey M. Floyd-Thomas, "Writing for Our Lives: Womanism as an Epistemological Revolution," in *Deeper Shades of Purple*, ed. Stacey M. Floyd-Thomas (New York: New York University Press, 2006), 2.

27. Diana L. Hayes, "Standing in the Shoes My Mother Made," in *Deeper Shades of Purple*, 56.

28. Cheryl A. Kirk-Duggan, "Quilting Relations with Creation," in *Deeper Shades of Purple*, 177.

29. Rosemarie Freeney Harding with Rachel Elizabeth Harding, "Hospitality, Haints, and Healing," in *Deeper Shades of Purple*, 99.

30. Michelle A. Gonzalez, "Who is Americana/o: Theological Anthropology, Postcoloniality, and the Spanish-Speaking Americas," in *Postcolonial Theologies: Divinity and Empire*, ed. Catherine Keller, Michael Nausner, and Mayra Rivera (St. Louis: Chalice, 2004), 58.

31. Ada María Isasi-Díaz, *Mujerista Theology* (Maryknoll, NY: Orbis Books, 1996).

32. Ibid., 113.

33. Ibid., 114.

34. Isasi-Díaz, *Mujerista Theology*, 128.

35. Ibid., 133.

36. Ibid.

37. Andrew Sung Park, *The Wounded Heart of God* (Nashville: Abingdon, 1993), 10.

38. Ibid., 38.

39. Ibid., 39–41.

40. Clara Sue Kidwell, Homer Noley, and George E. Tinker, *A Native American Theology* (Maryknoll, NY: Orbis Books, 2001), 85–86.

41. James H. Evans Jr., *We Have Been Believers* (Minneapolis: Fortress, 1992), 99.

42. Ibid.,107.

43. Evans, 115–16.

44. Justo L. González, *Mañana* (Nashville: Abingdon, 1990), 21.

45. Ibid., 22.

46. Ibid., 130.

47. Ibid., 133.

48. The section on white responses was eliminated in the revised volume, ostensibly to provide space to document other dimensions of early black theology.

49. See *Black Theology: A Documentary History, 1966–1979*, ed. Gayraud S. Wilmore and James H. Cone (Maryknoll, NY: Orbis, 1979), 135–237.

50. John C. Bennett, "Black Theology of Liberation," in *Black Theology: A Documentary History 1966–1979*, 181. To be sure, this is an argument that persists into the twenty-first century.

51. Frederick Herzog, "The Political Gospel," *The Christian Century*, (November 18, 1970), 1383.

52. Ibid.

53. Frederick Herzog, *Liberation Theology: Liberation in Light of the Fourth Gospel* (New York: Seabury, 1972), 15.

54. Ibid.

55. Ibid., 10.

56. Frederick Herzog, "The Liberation of White Theology," *The Christian Century*, (March 20, 1974), 319.

57. Ibid., 318.

58. Frederick Herzog, *God-Walk: Liberation Shaping Dogmatics* (Maryknoll, NY: Orbis, 1988), xxi.

59. Herzog, *Liberation Theology*, 63.

60. It is important to note that Herzog stresses that while human beings are made *imago Dei*, the corruption of our humanity means that we can only see and comprehend that image in the person of Jesus Christ. See *Liberation Theology*, 117ff.

61. Herzog, *Liberation Theology*, 145.

62. Ibid., 146.

63. Ibid., 158.

64. Ibid., 125.

65. Herzog, *God-Walk*, xxvi–xxvii.

66. Peter C. Hodgson, *New Birth of Freedom: A Theology of Bondage and Liberation* (Philadelphia: Fortress, 1976), xiii.

67. Ibid., xiv.

68. Ibid., 296–300.

69. Peter C. Hodgson, *God in History: Shapes of Freedom* (Minneapolis: Fortress, 1989), 47.

70. Peter C. Hodgson, *Winds of the Spirit: A Constructive Christian Theology* (Louisville: Westminster John Knox, 1994).

71. Ibid., 67.

72. Hodgson makes clear his interlocutors and indicates that they are woven throughout, even when "not specifically noted." *Winds of the Spirit*, 372n1.

73. Ibid., 197.

74. Daniel L. Migliore, *Faith Seeking Understanding*, 2nd ed. (Grand Rapids, MI: Eerdmans, 2004), 141.

75. Ibid., 142.

76. Ibid., 140, 153.

77. Karl Barth, *Ethics 1928–1929* (New York: Seabury, 1981), 128, quoted in Christopher Morse *Not Every Spirit: A Dogmatics of Christian Disbelief* (Valley Forge, PA: Trinity Press International, 1994), 256.

78. Morse, 257.

79. Ibid., 259–60.

80. Ibid., 284.

81. Karl Barth, *Ethics* (Edinburgh: T&T Clark, 1981), 164, quoted in Joerg Rieger, "Karl Barth," in *Beyond the Pale*, 163. Although their use of different editions may obscure this point, both Morse and Rieger are drawing upon the same publication.

82. McGrath, Alister. *Christian Theology: An Introduction*, 5th ed. (Malden, MA: Blackwell Publishing, 2011).

83. Serene Jones and Paul Lakeland, eds., *Constructive Theology: A Contemporary Approach to Classical Themes* (Minneapolis: Fortress, 2005).

3. Ashes to Ashes

An earlier and less developed version of this chapter appeared as the essay, "The Limits of Freedom," in *Alienation and Connection: Suffering in a Global Age* (Lanham, MD: Rowman Littlefield, 2011).

Epigraph. Carl Sandburg, "Four Preludes on Playthings of the Wind," in *The Complete Poems of Carl Sandburg* (New York: Harcourt Brace Jovanovich, 1969, 1970), 183.

Epigraph. Ronald Takaki, *A Different Mirror*, rev. ed. (New York: Little, Brown and Company, 1993, 2008), 3–4.

Epigraph. Maya Angelou, "Still I Rise," *Poems* (New York: Bantam Books, 1993), 154.

1. Mark A. Noll, *God and Race in American Politics* (Princeton: Princeton University Press, 2008), 12.

2. Forrest G. Wood, *The Arrogance of Faith* (Boston: Northeastern University Press, 1991; New York: Alfred A. Knopf, 1990), xviii. Citations refer to the Northeastern edition.

3. Cornel West, *Keeping Faith: Philosophy and Race in America* (New York: Routledge, 1993), 81.

4. Vine Deloria Jr., *God Is Red: A Native View of Religion*, 30th anniversary ed. (Golden, CO: Fulcrum Publishing, 2003).

5. Homer Noley, *First White Frost: Native Americans and United Methodism* (Nashville: Abingdon, 1991).

6. The Doctrine of Discovery was created by papal edict. It gave monarchs the right to appropriate nonchristian land by means of the conquest of nonchristian peoples.

7. Russell Thornton, *American Indian Holocaust and Survival* (Norman: University of Oklahoma Press, 1987), 43.

8. Ibid., 186.

9. Ibid., 69.

10. Thomas F. Gossett, *Race: The History of an Idea in America*, new ed. (New York: Oxford University Press, 1997), 17. First published in 1963.

11. Thornton, *American Indian Holocaust and Survival*, 5.

12. The infamous "Trail of Tears" of the Cherokee people witnessed the death of some 15,000 persons of the estimated 60,000 tribal members who made the forced march. See Stephen L. Pevar, *The Rights of Indians and Tribes* (New York: New York University Press), 304.

13. Thornton, *American Indian Holocaust and Survival*, 50.

14. *Chronicles of American Indian Protest* (Greenwich, CT: Fawcett, 1971), 7, cited in Noley, *First White Frost*, 22.

15. Pevar, *The Rights of Indians and Tribes*, 7–8.

16. Thornton, *American Indian Holocaust and Survival*, 43.

17. *The New York Public Library African American Desk Reference* (New York: John Wiley & Sons, 1999), 3.

18. John Hope Franklin and Alfred A. Moss Jr., *From Slavery to Freedom*, 7th ed. (New York: McGraw-Hill, 1994), 124.

19. *African American Desk Reference*, 33.

20. Takaki provides numerical evidence of the relationship of decreasing Indian land, increasing slave labor, and the exponential growth of cotton exports in *A Different Mirror*, 77.

21. Franklin and Moss, *From Slavery to Freedom*, 151.

22. Stacey Floyd-Thomas et al., *Black Church Studies: An Introduction* (Nashville: Abingdon, 2007), 6.

23. Ibid., 9.

24. Gossett, *Race: The History of an Idea in America*, 33.

25. Ibid., 35. Gossett notes that Linnaeus was little interested in the races, other than to classify the human species.

26. Ibid., 37, 38. Gossett goes on to indicate that Blumenbach coined the term "Caucasian," which was widely adopted, though "based upon a single skull in Blumenbach's collection which came from the Caucasian mountain region of Russia."

27. Ibid., 37. Buffon, however, believed that if Africans migrated to the north, the colder climate would lighten their skin. In this sense, race was not a fixed identity, but a function of geographical and other external factors.

28. Samuel Stanhope Smith, "An Essay on the Causes of the Variety of the Complexion and Figure in the Human Species," quoted in Gossett, *Race: The History of an Idea in America*, 40.

29. Gossett, *Race: The History of an Idea in America*, 41.

30. Ibid., 44. It bears noting that Jefferson also advocated the removal and destruction of Native peoples who could not or would not be civilized, i.e., adopt the white culture. See Takaki, *A Different Mirror*, 45–46.

31. Ibid., 53.

32. Ibid., 59.

33. Ibid., 62. Christians often subscribed to the monogenic theory as consistent with the biblical creation stories.

34. See, for example, Steven R. Haynes, *Noah's Curse: The Biblical Justification of American Slavery* (New York: Oxford University Press, 2002); Cain Hope Felder, *Race, Racism, and the Biblical Narratives* (Minneapolis: Fortress, 2002); and Daniel M. Goldenberg, *The Curse of Ham: Race and Slavery in Early Judaism, Christianity and Islam* (Princeton: Princeton University Press, 2003).

35. In 1868, the fourteenth amendment granted citizenship to children born in the United States without regard to their parents' racial identity. Children born in the United States of Asian descent were granted that right in 1898. Native Americans were not granted citizenship until early in the twentieth century.

36. Thornton, *American Indian Holocaust and Survival*, 105.

37. Ibid., 122.

38. Ibid., 123.

39. Report of Doolittle Committee, "Conditions of the Indian Tribes," cited in Francis Paul Prucha, *Documents of United States Indian Policy* (Lincoln: University of Nebraska Press, 1975), 102–3.

40. Prucha, *Documents of United States Indian Policy*, 104.

41. Pevar, *The Rights of Indians and Tribes*, 9.

42. Thornton, *American Indian Holocaust and Survival*, 152.

43. Ibid., 10–11.

44. Pevar, *The Rights of Indians and Tribes*, 278.

45. Abraham Lincoln, "Address on Colonization to the Deputation of Negroes (August 14, 1862) in *Lincoln on Race and Slavery*, ed. Henry Louis Gates Jr. (Princeton: Princeton University Press, 2009), 236.

46. Gates, *Lincoln on Race and Slavery*, 235.

47. Noll, *God and Race in American Politics*, 45.

48. Takaki, *A Different Mirror*, 141.

49. Contributing to the country through military service has always been a strategy toward full citizenship and privileges, though with mixed results. The armed services were segregated through World War II, and persons of color

found their status as veterans did little to change their treatment at home following the war.

50. Although the war with Mexico occurred prior to the Civil War and chronologically belongs in the first period of this survey, it is the aftermath of the war and the dehumanization of Mexicans that is our focus here. The racialized logic of the marginalization of Mexicans centers around neither the question of whether they are human nor the imperative to Christianize; rather it fits the second period's rationale of separate but equal and inferior to whiteness. Oddly, birth certificates of Latino/as in the United States will inscribe them as "white," meaning "not black," but their political, economic, social, and religious status will mark them as "not white."

51. Demographics taken from Lester G. Bugbee, "Slavery in Early Texas: I," *Political Science Quarterly* 13 (September 1898): 389–412, cited in Thomas J. Davis, *Race Relations in America: A Reference Guide with Primary Documents* (Westport, CT: Greenwood Press, 2006), 72.

52. Takaki, *A Different Mirror*, 156.

53. Ibid.

54. Ibid., 158.

55. Ibid., 163.

56. Ibid., 296.

57. Ibid., 305.

58. Ibid., 387.

59. Ibid., 180.

60. Ibid., 181.

61. Ibid., 188.

62. Ibid., 189.

63. Ibid., 343.

64. Noll, *God and Race in American Politics*, 25.

65. Ibid., 27

66. Frederick Douglass, "The Pro-Slavery Mob and the Pro-Slavery Ministry," *Douglass' Monthly* (March 1861), 417–18 cited in Noll, *God and Race in American Politics*, 41.

67. Noll, *God and Race in American Politics*, 76.

68. Gossett, *Race: The History of an Idea in America*, 180.

69. Ibid.

70. Ibid., 177.

71. Ibid., 178.

72. Ibid.

73. U.S. Bureau of Labor Statistics can be viewed and tracked under the "Employment Situation" in Archived News Releases at http://www.bls.gov/schedule/archives/all_nr.htm.

74. Marc Mauer and Ryan S. King, "Uneven Justice: State Rates of Incarceration by Race and Ethnicity," (The Sentencing Project, July 2007). This report can be accessed at http://www.sentencingproject.org/doc/publications/rd_stateratesofincbyraceandethnicity.pdf. See also, Michelle Alexander, *The New Jim Crow: Mass Incarceration in the Age of Colorblindness* (New York: The New Press, 2010).

75. Pevar, *The Rights of Indians and Tribes*, 3.

76. Derrick Bell, *Faces at the Bottom of the Well: The Permanence of Racism* (New York: Basic Books, 1992), v. Significantly, Bell acknowledges the serious economic disadvantages faced by many white Americans and suggests they (the poorer whites) prefer to protect "their sense of entitlement vis-á-vis blacks" than pursue changes to economic disparities by joining with persons of color (ibid., 7).

77. Ibid., 6.

78. Beth Frankel Merenstein, *Immigrants and Modern Racism: Reproducing Inequality* (Boulder: Lynne Reinner Publishers, 2008).

79. http://www.census.gov/prod/cen2010/briefs/c2010br-02.pdf

80. Historically black Protestant denominations are 92 percent black, though they have never prohibited whites from membership. The Pew Forum on Religion and Public Life, "U.S. Religious Landscape Survey," http://religions.pewforum.org/comparisons#4.

81. The race of twenty-four full-time faculty members was not available. Association of Theological Schools, "ATS Data Tables 2010–2011—Composition of Faculty and Compensation of Personnel," Table 3.1B Number of Full-Time Faculty by Race/Ethnicity, Rank, and Gender—United States, available online at http://www.ats.edu/Resources/PublicationsPresentations/Documents/AnnualDataTables/2010-11AnnualDataTables.pdf

4. Reformation

Epigraph. Ronald Takaki, *A Different Mirror*, rev. ed. (New York: Little, Brown and Company, 1993, 2008), 439.

Epigraph. Joy Harjo, "A Postcolonial Tale," in *The Woman Who Fell from the Sky* (New York: W. W. Norton, 1994), 18.

1. George Lipsitz, *How Racism Takes Place*, (Philadelphia: Temple University Press, 2011), 245.

2. W. E. B. Du Bois, "Of Our Spiritual Strivings," in *The Souls of Black Folks*, ed. Henry Louis Gates Jr. and Terri Hume Oliver (New York: W. W. Norton, 1999), 10–11.

3. Paul Tillich, *Systematic Theology*, vol. 1 (Chicago: University of Chicago Press, 1951), 31.

4. For a fuller analysis of Tillich's whiteness in the US context, see my essay in *Beyond the Pale: Reading Theology from the Margins*, ed. Stacey M. Floyd-Thomas and Miguel A. De La Torre (Louisville: Westminster John Knox, 2011), 151–60.

5. Lipsitz, *How Racism Takes Place*, 245.

6. Amartya Sen, *The Idea of Justice* (Cambridge, MA: The Belknap Press of Harvard University Press, 2009), 20.

7. Ibid.

CPSIA information can be obtained at www.ICGtesting.com
Printed in the USA
LVOW130225271012

304481LV00002B/4/P